ATTITUDE DETERMINES ALTITUDE

Elevate Your Mindset and Bring Success to Your Life

DR. KAROCKAS "DOC ROCK" WATKINS

Attitude Determines Altitude
by Dr. Karockas Watkins
© 2024 by Dr. Karockas Watkins. All rights reserved.

Editing by Adam Colwell's WriteWorks, LLC, Adam Colwell and Ginger Colwell
Cover and interior design by Clarity Designworks
Published by Dr. Karockas Watkins for "Doc Rock" through KDP and IngramSpark

Printed in the United States of America
ISBN (Paperback): 979-8-9900002-1-6
ISBN (Hardcover): 979-8-9900002-3-0
ISBN (eBook): 979-8-9900002-2-3

All rights reserved. Except in the case of brief quotations embodied in critical articles and reviews, no portion of this book may be reproduced, stored in a retrieval system, or transmitted in any form or by any means—electronic, mechanical, photocopy, recording, scanning, or other—without the prior written permission from the author. None of the material in this book may be reproduced for any commercial promotion, advertising or sale of a product or service.

While the author has made every effort to provide accurate internet addresses at the time of publication, neither the publisher nor the author assumes any responsibility for errors or for changes that occur after publication. Further, the publisher does not have any control over and does not assume any responsibility for author or third-party websites or their content.

CONTENTS

Acknowledgements v
Rise Toward a Greater, More Impactful Life vii
1 Attitude Defined 1
2 Attitude of Confidence 19
3 Attitude of Emotional Intelligence 35
4 Attitude of Money 47
5 Attitude of a Successful Leader 57
6 Attitude of Teamwork 71
Daily Devotion to Elevating Your Attitude 89

ACKNOWLEDGEMENTS

I'd like to thank the many people who have helped me learn and live for a cause bigger than myself throughout the years.

My special thanks to my editor and writing coach, Adam Colwell. I could not have done this without your help and encouragement to do this project.

Thanks to the leadership team of Emmanuel: The Connection Church. Also, special thanks to my spiritual mentor, the late Dr. Maurice K. Wright, who taught me to be a true leader. Thanks to Dr. Halton "Skip" Horton for your drive to be excellent at the highest level. Thanks to Dr. David Green Jr. You gave me the confidence to shoot for the moon.

I am grateful to my parents and in-laws for their support throughout the years. To my beautiful, lovely, committed wife, Audra, I appreciate what you do for our family and the sacrifices you have made. I am blessed to have three adult children and one son-in-law who love and encourage their father to be the best he can be. Thank you, Brianna, Christian, Joshua and Jonathan!

RISE TOWARD A GREATER, MORE IMPACTFUL LIFE

Everyone one of us has an attitude. Whether it's good, bad, or something in between, your attitude matters—but I have noticed that many people may not be aware of how their attitude plays a major part in their success in life.

Many people suffer from bad attitudes. I know I did. For example, when I was an engineering student at Kettering University, recognized as one of the toughest engineering schools in the country, my mindset was that I was average, while other students had an attitude of high achievement, no matter the cost.

My calculus teacher and mentor, Dr. David Green Jr., challenged me to believe that I could be one of the best. This caused me to begin developing my attitude toward dedication, grit, and success. Dedication means to never give up, no matter how hard it is or how bleak it looks, remaining committed to the end goal. Grit means to fight, to grind relentlessly with intensity and tenacity. Every morning, I had to have that attitude and walk in it, knowing that grit had to first occur in the mind before it could happen on the field. Success required fulfilling the mandate and purpose for my life. It was not doing what everyone else was, but what I had been meant to do, seeing it within myself and making it a reality.

Later, as a young engineer at International Business Machines Corporation (IBM), my attitude was again challenged by an IBM executive, Bob Dubose. He saw potential within me that my mindset had not yet recognized, and he wanted me to aspire to be at the top. I was doing good work, but he stretched me to think and do great work. To be stretched means to open up our minds to believe that we can do more, realizing the excellence inside of us, and seeing ourselves able to advance to a different, higher position. Great work requires putting in the time, energy, and research, after we have stretched ourselves, to get to the desired end goal.

Our attitude is determined by the way we see and handle situations from an emotional and mental perspective. Many, for example, view themselves from the stance of being a victim rather than a victor. I knew a gentleman who always saw himself as a failure. He'd blame others for what they thought about him and appropriate their thoughts as his own. I routinely talked to him about the power of mentally seeing himself as successful. I told him that if he could see his own success on the canvas of his imagination, he could have it. Doing this required forming a mental picture of where he could go, what he could be, or what he could have.

"You cannot have anything that you don't see," I said, "because it is a preview of a coming attraction and of what can possibly happen." I taught him that seeing his success allowed him to then form habits and disciplines to achieve that success. Today, that gentleman is doing well and running his own company that helps others get through life's crises.

Using the canvas of our imagination is often an act of faith. One night, a house caught fire and a young boy was forced to flee to the roof. The father stood on the ground below with outstretched arms, calling to his son, "Jump! I'll catch you." He knew the boy had to jump to save his life.

All the boy could see, however, was flames, smoke, and blackness. He was too afraid to leave the roof and leap into the unknown. His father kept yelling for him to jump, but the boy protested, "Daddy, I can't see you!"

The father yelled, "I know! But I can see you—and that's all that matters."

The boy closed his eyes, bravely envisioned his father holding him, and launched himself forward. The canvas of the boy's imagination became reality as his father caught him and took him safely away from the burning home.[1]

Others feel their attitude is expressed emotionally by getting sad or mad in certain situations, but our attitude is more than emotions and deeper than merely feeling down, angry, or frustrated. It's about how we see our lives, our goals, and our expectations when they are not being fulfilled. What we call depression or anger is really our attitude about our perceptions of what we have done or what we can do in the future. It's about whether we have control of those things, experience shortfalls, or are on target. The real issue is looking at what we have or have not accomplished in comparison to what we want to accomplish.

Once, I was very frustrated at where I was in my professional life. I felt that I had worked as hard as or harder than others, yet they seemed to be doing better than I was. I was playing a comparison game that I could not win. The more I looked at others, the angrier I got.

It wasn't until I changed my attitude about working, believing, and trusting in my own place and space that I gained any peace. I had to look at myself, and what I was doing, thinking, and saying, to understand that I wasn't trying to achieve or become what someone else was. I needed to focus on using my own talents, gifts, and passions and nothing more. I had to learn to be comfortable that the place I'd achieved and the space I'd occupied was exactly where I was supposed to be, even if the grass seemed greener on the other side. That allowed me to flourish.

Theodore Roosevelt, our nation's twenty-sixth president, rightly and famously said, "Comparison is the thief of joy." If we are going to judge ourselves, our actions, or where we are at any given point, we do not need to compare ourselves to others. We judge according to what we know, who we know we are, and what we know we can do—and all of that is informed by what we are meant to do and be. In 1884, a young man died, and after the funeral, his grieving parents felt they should establish a memorial to their son. Determined and confident in who they were and what they could do, they met the president of Harvard University. After they expressed their desire to fund a memorial, the college president dismissed their request. "Perhaps you have in mind a scholarship instead?"

"No," the mother replied, "we were thinking of something more substantial than that—perhaps a building."

The president of Harvard brushed aside the idea as being too expensive, and the couple departed. It wasn't until the following year that the beleaguered president learned that the couple had gone west and established a then-massively priced $26 million memorial they named Leland Stanford Junior University—better known today as Stanford University.[2] Their undaunted attitude certainly paid off in honoring their son with an enduring legacy.

Attitude thrives off of a positive mindset fed by a proper perspective, and lots of people seemingly want to be on top, successful, and in control. But they'll never get there when their mindset is on the bottom. Perhaps they don't want to work hard, failing to understand the many sacrifices that must happen in order to be on top. It could be that they accept failure as final, so that mindset keeps them thinking like someone at the bottom who is unsuccessful in fulfilling their goals, missions, and dreams in life.

Joe Theismann enjoyed an illustrious career as quarterback of the Washington Redskins (today's Washington Commanders). He led the team to two Super Bowl appearances, winning in 1983 before losing the following year. When an infamous leg injury, incurred during a nationally-televised game in 1985, forced him out of football, he was Washington's all-time leading passer. However, Theismann had a confession about the season after winning his first and only Super Bowl title. "I got stagnant," he admitted. "I thought the team revolved around me. I should have known it was time to go when I didn't care whether or not a pass hit (wide receiver) Art Monk in the '8' or the '1' on his uniform. My approach had changed. I was gripping about the weather, my shoes, practice times—everything."

He then said, "Today I wear my two rings—the winner's ring from Super Bowl XVII and the loser's ring from Super Bowl XVIII. The difference between those two rings lies in applying oneself and not accepting anything but the best."[3] What happened? His mindset had regressed from the top to the bottom, and it ultimately made him less successful.

Such complacency is a blight that saps your energy, causes a drain on your brain, and dulls your attitude. The first symptom is satisfaction with things as they are. The second is the rejection of things as they might be. "Good enough" becomes today's watchword and tomorrow's standard in your life. Complacency makes people fear the unknown, mistrust the untried, and abhor the new. Like water, complacent people follow the easiest course: downhill. They draw false strength from looking back.[4] In other words, they do not challenge themselves intellectually to the point where they change their mindset. They are not open to expect or to do something differently. They are willing to receive and get what they can out of an experience, but they don't have the proper attitude that thinks about how they can take what they are seeing to move toward success or give back to others.

A great attitude is a mentality that is put into action.

In the end, your attitude is in direct proportion to your *altitude*. Swiss psychiatrist and balloonist Bertrand Piccard became the first person, along with colleague Brian Jones, to complete a non-stop balloon flight around the globe. Piccard was quoted in National Geographic about the similarity he sees between balloon flight and daily life.

"In the balloon, you are prisoners of the wind, and you go only in the direction of the wind," he said. "In life, people think they are prisoners of circumstance. But in the balloon, as in life, you can change altitude, and when you change altitude, you change direction. You are not a prisoner anymore."[5]

Our attitude changes our altitude and dictates our outlook. If I have an attitude that I won't be the best, that will drive me not to be promoted, go higher in my field, or create something new. I cannot go any higher than what I am thinking. On the flip side, if I am living in the projects, but I can see myself owning a home, driving a nice car, and doing things that others may not be able to do because my attitude will drive me to do whatever is necessary to achieve those goals.

That's what I did. Even though I was in a situation that may not have been favorable, my attitude allowed me to change my altitude and rise toward a greater, more impactful life.

How we choose to think—our mindset—will not only affect what we expect from life, but it'll impact what we do in life.

> A great attitude is a mentality that is put into action.

I wrote *Attitude Determines Altitude* to encourage those who are pursuing life with the proper attitude, and to transform those who have been struggling with having the proper and necessary attitude to succeed. After reading this book, I hope your mind will think and your mouth will say, "Bring it on, world! I can do it!"

1
ATTITUDE DEFINED

*An attitude continually transformed by
your mindset will bring success to your life.*

You are where you are today based on the attitudes you had in the past, and who you will be in the future is based on the attitudes you have today. Better stated, you are today what you thought yesterday, and you will be tomorrow what you are thinking today.

Your attitude controls your success and failure—and it is time for it to give you more success.

Success, however, is not just the acquisition of material things or professional status. *Success is the accomplishment of an aim or purpose.* I discovered this to be true when I saw myself gaining some things that I never had but still being unfulfilled. It felt good in the moment, but there was no longevity to that feeling.

As I asked myself, *What is this?* I realized that fulfillment comes when we achieve or accomplish who we are called to be on this earth.

I believe every person has the right to a successful life.

This requires you to discover your "why." It is the reason you exist, your purpose for living. Until you figure it out, you'll always think about the "how" and the "when," but never realize them.

Many times, our why is born from our gifts, talents, and struggles, and it is perhaps best seen as that one thing, if we had all the money in the world, that we would do for free. I tell people that their why is that thing that will get them out of the bed when everyone else is still hitting the snooze button.

When we discover our why, we will search diligently to recognize how to accomplish it, and we will wait as long as it takes to gain the knowledge, stability, and experience to fulfill it. Then, the question of when our why happens is swallowed up in the journey of understanding it.

When I work with clients to help them discover their why, I ask them questions such as, "What is your passion?" "What is your educational background?" "What comes easy to you?" "What excites you?" I teach them that their why shouldn't be something that is done just for money, because when they find out what they are meant to do, they'll never "work" a day in their lives. Living out their why will require work and lots of it, but it won't feel like work. Therefore, if they are complaining about what they do, are stressed out about it, or simply don't want to do it any longer, it wasn't their why to begin with. Their why, instead, will be based on their passion, and it will feed their commitment to it over the long haul.

When we know our why, it shifts us to a positive place—one where we can be continually transformed by our mindset—because we know our purpose and have that thing in front of us that drives our emotions to be stable and to grow.

Times past

Growing up in the projects, government housing in a small town in Alabama, I didn't see many people who knew their why or had an attitude of success. What I did see were attitudes of religion, tradition, and mediocrity that were rooted in survival.

I was a church kid, and I loved going to church. Later as a boy, I'd travel with my stepfather, Dr. George Franklin, as he went and preached in country churches. Everyone from my family to my friends religiously went to church, but I didn't see anything that showed me they were really focusing on an attitude of success. Church was just something they did on Sunday, but after that, they went back to the same old mindset of survival.

They had the attitude that good existed, but they were not expecting that good in their lives.

I reasoned, *I don't want to be a part of that.*

At the same time, I saw many traditions that didn't seem to be helping anyone grow as people. These traditions seemed well and good on the surface: being nice to our neighbors, singing in the choir, or our church family helping one another. But they were done in a way that enabled the survival mindset rather than allowing people to move beyond it.

With mediocrity, I saw people who were average. My definition of average is to be "on top of the bottom," and that's all everyone wanted. They didn't want to get all the way to the very top. I'd hear, "I'm gonna work, but I'm not going to go overboard," or, "I'm not going to extend myself in order to be my best."

But I don't want to be better than anyone else, I believed. *I want to be the best Karockas I can be.*

They settle. They're comfortable.
I want to be more.

I'm thankful I was able to see beyond what was shown to me so that I could envision goodness and success for my life. This happened in a simple yet incredible way when I was just seven years old.

Every summer, I stayed with my biological father's mother, Mama Sally, while my mother and stepfather spent more time with my two younger siblings, Brandon and Ashia. Mama Sally lived across town from where we did, only 15 minutes away, but her home was in the older projects while mine was in a government-assisted home that, while in slightly better condition, was still project housing. My biological father and I often went fishing during those summers, and Mama Sally usually joined us on those hot, summer mornings out on the Tennessee River.

My Mama Sally and I were very close. Even as a boy, I admired her hard work and entrepreneurship. She made Bee-Bops, Kool-Aid that is mixed and then frozen in cups, and sold them, along with pickled eggs, pickled bologna, homemade chocolate and vanilla cupcakes, and Little Debbie cakes to kids and adults in the neighborhood. I helped her shop during the week, and I assisted as she cleaned up the house, all of which brought us together.

As I did each evening, I was sitting at the table by the open window in her small, beige-painted kitchen, hoping to catch a breeze to cool the humidity that still pressed in even after the sun was setting. In the waning light, I could see the outline of the clotheslines against the darkening sky and the silhouette of the barrel grill in the small backyard.

One particular night, I watched as Mama Sally made watermelon flavored Bee-Bops. She was very neat, so the only things out were what she needed at the moment: Kool-Aid, a jug, and a lot of white, pure cane sugar. It smelled so good! She often let me sample a spoonful to see if it was sweet enough.

Mama Sally put them in the freezer that covered one entire wall of the kitchen, and when she went into another room to do something else—I had an epiphany. It was as though God Himself sat down across from me at the kitchen table to have a conversation.

"You have favor on your life. You are going to do great things to literally touch the world. Not just in Alabama, but in the world. So, walk in a place of discipline to get good grades and do what is right. Don't fear any other people of different races or in different cultures. One is no better than the other. They are all different, and you are going to be used in their lives in a special way."

That moment was incredible and so real that I remember it today in such rich detail.

> You have favor on your life. You are going to do great things to literally touch the world.

Prior to that night, my attitude was that of a loser and a failure. I looked at my physical, social, and economic conditions as if they were what *I* was. Physically, I was smaller, slower, and uncoordinated compared to all the other boys who were good in sports. I was the cream puff, always the last person to get picked for the team. Socially, I was a little awkward. I liked reading, fishing, and being around older people and listening to them, so I was different than most of the guys around me. They were getting into trouble, and I wasn't. Economically, we lived in the projects. My mother and stepfather worked, but we just didn't have what most everybody else did. I thought we were not successful, and I knew I didn't want to live in subsidized housing when I was older.

Most people are products of their environment, but they can even be from a decent physical environment and still have no hope. Most of my aunts and uncles from my mother's side were on government assistance and codependent on one another. None of them graduated from high school. They had negative attitudes about life, education, and finances. Their mindset was, "I don't have anything, so don't ask me for anything. We are poor."

But when I heard those words in my heart and mind about favor and the great things I was going to do, they addressed my physical, social, and economic conditions. They let me know that I was not a loser. I was not a failure. I had greatness within me. I had been given a vision that I would work with people of other races to achieve greatness.

My attitude began to change, and as it did, so did my life. I went from making failing scores in the first grade to being one of the top students in my elementary school. In fifth grade, Miss Pat O'Shield pushed me so that when I was in middle school, I wanted to be the best. My seventh-grade teacher, Miss Constantine Pope, pushed me even further. Neither one let me settle for being lowly. They had me thinking that I was the best and that I could achieve and *be* the best. That carried me successfully through high school, earning me a sponsorship with the General Motors Company to attend what was then the GMI Engineering and Management Institute (now Kettering University) in Flint, Michigan.

There, my attitude on life was challenged once again. It came in a most unexpected way from my college roommate, Michael Harris. He was making A's in his engineering classes while I was making B's. One morning at our apartment, I asked him to come to church with me. I was scheduled to preach the 11:00 a.m. Sunday morning message for the first time ever, and I was very excited about the opportunity.

Always unapologetic, he was not at all hesitant to respond.

"You want to go preach and do all the Bible says you can do and all that," he said, "but you don't believe it yourself because I make A's and you make B's, and you are just as intelligent as I am. You don't have confidence, so I'm not going to listen to you. Until your grades reflect what you are saying, I don't want to hear you."

Michael's candor made me mad—yet all the way to church, I was thinking, *He is right.*

As I calmed down, I began to consider what I needed to do to change. Not surprisingly, it began with my mindset. I had to start seeing things differently. I realized that I thought I had arrived when, in reality, I hadn't. *I've got to work on this. I can make A's. Why am I not making A's? What is stopping me from being my best?*

From that day onward, I began studying harder than I ever had before. I worked on refining my talents. I received the added encouragement I mentioned earlier from Dr. Green and applied it. Within a semester, the B's went to A's—and within that same semester, Michael saw what was going on, and he did go with me to church to hear me preach. Today, he lives in Buffalo, New York, and he and his family visit me in Alabama every year.

I am grateful Michael boldly challenged me to change my mindset and take my attitude to a higher place. I graduated with a mechanical engineering degree and earned honors on my thesis because of that transformation and elevation of my attitude, and I now have a master's degree, two doctorates, and a certificate in business excellence. I own a leadership consulting company, I am chief executive officer of a leading nonprofit business, and I am on a team of cultural leadership consultants with a major insurance broker where I travel, teach, and train others around the world.

My why—to empower, lead, and teach people to reach their goals by helping them to maximize their potential—is being fulfilled.

Attitude and philosophy

I believe millions of people fall short of the best for their lives because of a lack of excellence in their attitude or personal philosophy of success and growth.

Philosophy is derived from two words: *philo-*, meaning "to love," and *-osophy*, meaning "to think." So, our philosophy is simply "loving the way we think." That philosophy has been shaped by our history, the direct and indirect teachings we've received, our financial and social status, and other influences.

Chinese philosopher, Zeng Shen, was young enough to be Confucius' grandson, yet he won high praise from Confucius himself and later taught Zisi, the grandson of Confucius. One of Zeng Shen's famous philosophies goes as follows: "Every day I ask myself three questions. The first is, 'Have I sinned in my thoughts and actions toward others?' The second is, 'Have I broken faith in any of my friendships?' The third is, 'Have I tried to teach anything to others I have not fully learned and understood myself?'"

If Zeng Shen asked himself these three questions every day, resolving to make no mistakes, then, young as he was, we can well understand why Confucius honored and trusted him. Not only is each of the three questions extremely important in themselves, but the practice of examining one's own behavior every day is a habit that every person should cultivate.[6] Life and peace come when we have an attitude where we are careful to check what we are saying, doing, and hearing in every area of our lives.

A person's mental attitude has an almost unbelievable effect on both physical and psychological ability. The British psychiatrist, J.A. Hadfield, provided a striking illustration of this fact in his booklet, *The Psychology of Power*. "I asked three people," he wrote, "to submit themselves to test the effect of mental suggestion on their strength, which was measured by gripping a dynamometer." He set up three different conditions in which they were to grip the dynamometer with all their strength. First, he tested them under normal conditions. The average grip was 101 pounds. Next, he tested them after he had hypnotized them and told them that they were very weak. Their average grip dramatically decreased to only 29 pounds. In the third test, Dr. Hadfield told them under hypnosis that they were very strong. Their average grip jumped to 142 pounds.[7]

Attitude, then, is the mental agent that causes us to comprehend, see, and handle situations and circumstances in a certain way. It can be seen as the glasses through which we see the world. It controls the choices we make, the opportunities we pursue, the money we earn, and the success we achieve.

Attitude even plays a significant role in how we read, meditate, and perform. If we don't have the right attitude when we read, it is easy to criticize what we are reading, finding something wrong with every little thing that we consume. If we read with a positive attitude, though, we'll view it from a victor's standpoint. We'll find something, that one good nugget, that will help us go forward with our goals, dreams, and pursuits in life. When I first read *Emotional Intelligence 2.0*, coauthored by Travis Bradbury and Jean Greaves, I had a negative attitude about the notion that someone's emotional intelligence (EQ) was what made them successful as opposed to their IQ, or intelligence quotient. I thought good old-fashioned smarts was most important. But as I opened myself up and viewed the subject of EQ through the lens of research, I quickly saw that EQ was both positive and beneficial. Not only did I go on to learn more about emotional intelligence, but I also became certified to facilitate EQ seminars, which I've now done around the world. Later, I have dedicated an entire section of this book to how EQ ties with having an attitude that determines your altitude.

> Attitude is the mental agent that causes us to comprehend, see, and handle situations.

Meditation is where verbalization, visualization, and internalization are used to focus our thoughts to see and rehearse the actions we want. These three forms of meditation encompass and address the basic components of an experience shaped by words spoken out loud, emotions felt as real, and images seen on the canvas of the imagination. If we don't have the right attitude when we meditate, we can be very judgmental of ourselves and others, all "woe is me" and venting in nature. Meditation cannot be done out of rote ritual, or just to see if we will get what we want. Instead, meditation should be done with an attitude of seeking more peace of mind and insight about what we can have and what is in store for us in the future. That's when our meditations become more dynamic and effectual as we start to see them come to fruition.

An interesting perspective on performance comes from Denis Waitley, the gifted motivational speaker, consultant, and author of the audio series, "The Psychology of Winning," and books such as *Seeds of Greatness* and *The Winner's Edge.* He said, "The winner glories in the good; the whiner majors in the mediocre. Winners' thinking processes differ from other people's. As part of their normal, moment-to-moment stream of consciousness, winners think constantly in terms of 'I can' and 'I will.' Losers concentrate their waking thoughts on … what they should have done … would have done … what they can't do."

Waitley concluded, "When the mind's self-talk is positive, performance is more likely to be successful. The huge majority of our negative doubts and fears are imaginary or beyond our control."[8]

In addition, many people have gifts, degrees, and skills, but the reason they don't achieve their life goals is because they don't have a positive mental attitude about things such as their self-image. Years ago, there was a company that received a less than acceptable grade in their annual certification audit. The organization had talented individuals and a good management staff, but they were focused more on their skill sets than their mindsets.

Top leadership challenged everyone to go from "good to great," using the book of the same name by Jim Collins. Changes were implemented in operations, policies and procedures, and overall work culture. As a result, the staff's mindset was elevated, and they became a unified team that was more productive and efficient. The next audit confirmed a 100-percent improvement in all facets of the company.

Contrary to what many people may assume, attitude is not always vocal or loud. It can be quiet but have loud results. I was involved in a situation with a city Chamber of Commerce where it wanted to take on a greater role when it came to diversity and equity in the community's culture. A lot of chamber members were opinionated about what we should do, how we should do it, and who should do it. But my attitude was to assess what was going on, view what we needed to do from the standpoint of the chamber's overall mission, and determine how I could help achieve that. As a result, without being the loudest person in the room, I became the chairman of the diversity, equity, and inclusion task force, and some very positive things have resulted from that role.

There was another occasion when a company wanted to do something internally to address racial equality. I met with one of its leaders who told me it was hard for them to find people of color to work in their institution. I suggested they could create such opportunities on their own, and I helped them set up a program with the business school at Alabama A&M University. Through this program, the company would hire two students to intern with them and become a part of their company, and it has been successful.

So, attitude can be managed and manifested in a variety of ways—but in the end, it is the part of our mental capacity that controls how we think and look at things.

Attitude and how our mind functions

In the Hebrew language, the word "heart" is interpreted as being the center of human thought and spiritual life. We tend to look at the heart as being the seat of our emotions, but in ancient cultures, the heart was also the seat of intelligence. The mind and heart, therefore, are one in the sense of *thought*.

I believe humans are tripartite in nature. Each one of us is composed of body, soul, and spirit. Our bodies are temporal. Our spirits are eternal. Our souls are the place where our mind resides—and our mind can be broken up into three compartments: the conscious, the subconscious, and our conscience. All three are involved in transforming our mindset to change the altitude of our attitude.

Let's look at each one.

The conscious mind is where our purposeful thoughts, as well as our initial reasoning and logical thinking, take place.

The subconscious mind is the autopilot of the conscious mind and has the responsibility to automatically carry out the finished work of the conscious mind. When our conscious mind has accepted certain norms and values as truth, it is then the subconscious mind that takes that thought and handles our decision-making so that the conscious mind is freed up to receive and process new data.

Our conscience is our belief system containing ethical and moral principles that control or inhibit our actions or thoughts according to our sense of right or wrong. In order for us to become successful people, our conscience must be transformed. This requires a disciplined process of applying new truths to our lives. These new truths are learned from our beliefs and our experiences. They can also come from books such as this one, credible authority figures, and seminars that are not contradictory to our beliefs.

To prepare our heart and mind to have an elevated attitude, we must continually make three essential decisions.

1. We must die to self.
This concept mandates that we lose sight of our own interests, forget them entirely, and place the interests of others first.

This positions us to deny our own selfish ambitions. That doesn't mean we cannot have goals, but it does mean those goals must be aligned with what benefits others, not just something we desire.

As a boy, I had always wanted to be a medical doctor. I would read my mom's nursing books, and I took all the science classes I could in high school. One day, while I was contemplating how to get into and pay for medical school, I visited a doctor. He was my mother's colleague, so I knew he would be a great person to give some good advice and serve as a sounding board for my goals.

He explained that he became a doctor because he felt God had "called" him to go into that field. Furthermore, he said his practice was successful because he was doing what God wanted him to do. He counseled me to do the same, and if the medical field was where I was supposed to be, I'd know it. The doctor was aware of my grades and my capabilities, but he told me to return to him for help becoming a doctor only after I knew for sure that was my future direction.

Let me tell you, I had to do some dying to self after that conversation. I knew what I had heard when I was a boy about the favor that was on my life. I just had to confirm my path.

I never made it back to that doctor—but I have been richly blessed as I died to self and decided to empower, lead, and teach people to reach their goals by helping them to maximize their potential.

> **I have been richly blessed as I died to self.**

2. We must die to our weaknesses.
In our reasoning and thought processes, our weaknesses will naturally fight against what we have decided to do, waging war against our elevated attitude, causing it to grow weary and stagnant.

Early in my professional career, there were times I wanted my name to be everywhere. I desired fame and fortune, and I wanted it right away. I didn't want to wait or work for it. I didn't want it even to help people. I wanted it because it was what *I* wanted. My ego and selfish ambition were weaknesses—and they had to die. I had to commit to myself that fame wasn't important. My name didn't need to be everywhere. The only thing that really mattered was serving people.

As I killed those weaknesses, helping others became most important to me. That has allowed me to fulfill the words of the genius theoretical theorist, Albert Einstein. "Try not to become a man of success, but rather try to become a man of value."

3. We must die to the expectations of society.
Developing an elevated attitude based on a transformed mindset starts by dying to the way society sees success.

There was a time early in my career when I was trying to advance as a young engineer at General Motors. My attitude was simple: get there by any means necessary as long as I didn't do anything illegal. I picked up that mentality at Kettering, where we were taught to be cut-throat in everything we did. Therefore, I wasn't taking into account the feelings and needs of others, and I certainly wasn't a team player. I was in it for myself. That was how society did things.

Then I was challenged by a seasoned engineer about my goals and plans for the future. He told me I was not displaying the right attitude, and he taught me about being a servant leader: a person who can have goals and dreams, but who puts other people and his team first. He helped me to understand that what I wanted to achieve could only be done with the aid of my colleagues. As someone once said, "If you live your life as if everything is about you, you will be left with just that. Just you."

I didn't want that, and I took his advice. As I went to work on a new project, a specific machine for operations, I consulted with everybody on that line. I listened to their ideas and applied them. I asked, "What do you believe will make this work?" "How can I help you achieve that?" I made it about *them*.

When it was time to present the machine to the top brass from headquarters, I declared that we, the team, did it. We accomplished it together.

I got more accolades for that project than anything I had done up to that point. Why? Because I killed society's view of how to be successful and became a servant leader. I chose to esteem others greater than myself.

Dying to ourselves, our weaknesses, and to society's expectations takes unwavering commitment. In his book, *In the Eye of the Storm*, author Max Lucado told an incredible story set in the operating room of Kane Summit Hospital in New York City on February 15, 1921. There, a doctor was performing an appendectomy. In many ways, the events leading up to the surgery were uneventful. The patient had complained of severe abdominal pain, and the diagnosis was clear: an inflamed appendix. Dr. Evan O'Neill Kane was performing the surgery, and in his distinguished 37-year medical career, he had done nearly 4,000 appendectomies—and this surgery would be uneventful in all ways except two.

The first novelty was the use of local anesthesia in major surgery. Dr. Kane was a crusader against the hazards of general anesthesia. He contended that a local application was far safer. Many of his colleagues agreed with him in principle, but in order for them to agree in practice, they had to see the theory applied. Dr. Kane searched for a patient willing to undergo the surgery while under local anesthesia, and the appendectomy patient made himself available.

The patient was prepped and wheeled into the operating room, and the local anesthetic was applied. As he had done many times before, Dr. Kane dissected the superficial tissues and located the appendix. He skillfully excised it and concluded the surgery. During the procedure, the patient complained only of minor discomfort. The volunteer was taken into post-op, then placed in a hospital ward. He recovered quickly and was dismissed two days later.

Dr. Kane had proven his theory. He demonstrated that local anesthesia was a viable, and even preferable, alternative. Lucado wrote, "But I said there were two facts that made the surgery unique. I've told you the first: the use of local anesthesia. The second is the patient. The courageous candidate for surgery by Dr. Kane was Dr. Kane."[9]

Dr. Kane operated on himself! Talk about unwavering commitment! The doctor became the patient in order to convince the patients to trust the doctor.

Sometimes, we need to operate on ourselves to die to the things that will elevate our attitude.

Both an eagle and a chicken are classified as birds. They have wings, and each one can elevate off the surface of the earth. But we can distinguish that a certain bird is an eagle because an eagle flies high on mountain cliffs, will fly into the storm toward the sun, and demands respect as it searches for its prey. A chicken, on the other hand, only flies as high as the barnyard fence. It plucks with its head down toward the ground when looking for food. Its power is trivial compared to the eagle.

I like the chicken, but I am thankful for the wings of an eagle. I don't want to hang out with chickens. I eat chickens. I want to hang out with eagles because they soar high, and I want to fly like one.

That requires confidence—an elevated attitude that we'll explore next.

2
ATTITUDE OF CONFIDENCE

*Be strong and courageous
in your thoughts and actions.*

Frank Lloyd Wright is among the most innovative architects in American history. But his fame wasn't limited to the United States. About 100 years ago, officials in Japan asked Wright to design a hotel for Tokyo that would be capable of surviving an earthquake. When the architect visited Japan to see where the Imperial Hotel was to be built, he was appalled to find only about eight feet of earth on the site. Beneath that was 60 feet of soft mud that slipped and shook like jelly. Every test hole he dug filled up immediately with water.

A lesser man probably would have given up right there. But not Frank Lloyd Wright. Since the hotel was going to rest on fluid ground, Wright decided to build it like a ship. Instead of trying to keep the structure from moving during a quake, he incorporated features that would allow the hotel to ride out the shock without damage. Supports were sunk into the mud, and sections of the foundation were cantilevered from the supports. The rooms were built in sections like a train and hinged together. Water pipes and electric lines, usually the first to shear off in an earthquake, were hung in vertical shafts where they could sway freely if necessary.

Wright also knew that the major cause of destruction after an earthquake was fire because water lines are apt to be broken in the ground, leaving no way to put out a fire. So, he insisted on adding a large outdoor pool in the courtyard of his hotel "just in case."

It took courage to justify and design such a unique structure, but Wright saw it through. Then, on September 1, 1923, Tokyo experienced the greatest earthquake in its history up to that time. There were fires all over the city, and 140,000 people perished. In the U.S., news reports were slow to come in. One newspaper wanted to print the story that the Imperial Hotel had been destroyed, as rumor had it. But when a reporter called Frank Lloyd Wright, he said that they could print the story if they wished, but they would only have to retract it later. He was confident the hotel would not collapse.

Shortly afterward, Wright got a telegram from Japan. The Imperial Hotel was completely undamaged. Not only that—it had provided a temporary home for hundreds of people. When the fires that raged all around the hotel threatened to spread, bucket brigades kept the structure wetted down with water from the hotel's pool.

The Imperial Hotel isn't there anymore. It was torn down in the 1960s to be replaced by a more modern structure.[10] But the legacies of the hotel's strength and Wright's courage to boldly see to its construction remain today.

To have an Attitude of Confidence, we must develop our strength and courage to hold fast to what we have purposed for our lives. Many people have attitudes of fear and weakness because they do not renew their minds in the areas of boldness and power. Yet true confidence only comes from elevating our attitude so that our thoughts and actions reflect that confidence.

Attitude is the father of behavior

No amount of training in leadership skills, courses in management methods, power titles, promotions, or associations can be a substitute for having the right attitude. Attitude is the power of visualized victory, and this mindset is a natural by-product of the integration of our self-worth, self-esteem, and sense of value or significance.

Incredibly, the average person has as many as 60,000 thoughts a day—and the vast majority of them, 80 percent, are negative. You can offset this trend in your thinking by emotionally esteeming your current goals and your future expectations about them above your present reality. See it, believe it, and act as if it has already happened. Tell yourself, "Yes, I can! I can feel this way. I deserve to feel this way!"

> **Attitude is the power of visualized victory.**

Self-worth encompasses your attitude as it is impacted by emotional states such as pleasure, triumph, pride, despair, shame, and pain. In their 2007 article on the Rosenberg Self-Esteem Scale Greek Validation on Student Sample, Eliot R. Smith and Diane M. Mackie explained that "self-concept is what we think about the self; self-esteem is the positive or negative evaluations of the self, as in how we feel about it."[11]

Our self-esteem is elevated when we contribute to our society with importance and meaning. When the COVID-19 pandemic first broke out, many people in our community in northern Alabama suffered from a lack of food. They were from all races and all ages, all demographics and all socio-economic backgrounds, and I had never seen anything like it before. When I saw them standing in line for hours hoping to receive food and household supplies from a Christian ministry in Huntsville, it broke my heart and moved me to action. Ability Plus Inc. in Huntsville, the largest single provider of services for people with special needs in Alabama, and Emmanuel: The Connection Church partnered to give out food boxes one Saturday morning. In all, we gave away a couple thousand boxes of non-perishable food: nuts, rice, cereal, and beans. It was hard, but incredibly rewarding, work. As we demonstrated love and cared for others, many people were blessed. Self-esteem is affirmed when you think and feel good about yourself.

Finally, our sense of value or significance is elevated when we see our uniqueness and great worth. Violins made by masters like Antonio Stradivari produce an incomparably beautiful sound and sell for millions to investors. But excellent violins are not like works of art, to be hung on a wall or displayed under glass. They'll lose their tone if not played regularly, and they actually increase in value the more they're used. That's why the Stradivari Society exists. It puts those first-rate violins into the hands of great violin virtuosos to ensure the instruments are preserved, cared for, and played. The musicians are even required to give the violin owners two command performances each year. As you change your mindset about yourself, you will become a virtuoso at whatever you do and in whatever obstacle you face. In fact, your attitude should be the attitude of a king. You must think to rule, not over individuals, but over situations.

In essence, our attitude is the manifestation of who we think we are, for good or for bad. Attitude dictates our responses to the present and determines the quality of our future. To put it more personally, you are your attitude, and your attitude is you. If you do not control your attitude, it will control you. It will propel you forward or knock you backward. Attitude is always the father of behavior—and when you elevate your mindset, confidence and success will follow.

Attitude also determines your success or failure in any venture in life. More opportunities have been lost, withheld, or forfeited because of a poor attitude than from anything else. More powerful than the pain of the past or the confusion of the present, the right attitude and the confidence it brings can turn darkness to light and make small become big.

Attitude directly impacts our decisions, the *quality* of our commitment to those decisions, and how well we *remain* committed to those decisions. Decision-making is a product of our attitude since our attitude helps to form opinions and ideas in daily living. When we are in the process of making a decision, our mindset will determine our choices.

There are six attitudes that produce failure. Let's briefly look at each one.

1. Arrogance is defined as an attitude of superiority manifested in an overbearing manner or in presumptuous claims or assumptions. When we have an arrogant attitude, we fail to listen to constructive criticism and knowledge from others. Many times, this hinders us from making vital decisions that'll cause us to mature personally or help in the strategic growth of an organization.

2. Judgmentalism is an attitude that forms opinions about others that are usually harsh and critical in nature. This leads to failure because it negatively affects solid relationships and alienates people. Such relationship bankruptcy leaves us without the support we need to grow and move to higher levels in our goals and career.

3. Boastfulness is an expression of excessive self-pride. This attitude causes us to not fully look at ourselves and keeps us from seeing the negative traits or behaviors that we need to improve to avoid failure.

4. Comparison is judging ourselves based on what others are thinking or doing. Events such as a promotion, a divorce, an empty nest, or retirement can cause us to inspect who we are in relation to someone else. This can leave us feeling insecure, anxious, or confused. This is not a healthy mindset and can lead to a slow decline of our self-esteem.

5. Negative competition is when we compete with others in such a way that we want to win by any means necessary, even at the expense of others. This attitude shuts down the trust and psychological safety of a team, and negatively impacts the overall culture of an organization, eating away at teamwork and relationships.

6. Disobedience is an attitude where we refuse to obey rules or authority. This gives ground to undisciplined actions and leads to systemic failures. Disobedience is dangerous, in that we may feel like we are succeeding when, in reality, destruction is just down the road.

Conversely, there are seven attitudes that lead to success.

1. Humility is the quality of being humble, and it puts the needs of other people before our own as we think of others ahead of ourselves. This does not draw attention to us, and it can mean acknowledging that we are not always right. When we have this attitude, we allow others to achieve their best by not trying to upstage or grandstand anyone else.

2. Teachableness means we are ready to learn and open our hearts to new ideas, pursuits, and dreams. Having this attitude means we are willing to do whatever is necessary to gain knowledge on a particular subject, allowing us to stay on the top of our profession or excel in our personal lives.

3. Compassion is an emotional response to sympathy and creates within us a desire to help others. It encourages us to see a need and not just give lip service to it, but actually take action toward solving it. It is an attitude that pulls people together to unite around a cause.

4. Generosity is the willingness to give of our time and our finances to benefit the recipient. Positive things happen when we give of ourselves. Author, salesperson, and motivational speaker, the late Zig Zigler, said, "You can have everything in life you want, if you will just help other people get what they want." An attitude of generosity causes us to be sacrificial, which aids in our maturity and leads to greater success in life.

5. Diligence is described by author Steven K. Scott in *The Richest Man Who Ever Lived: King Solomon's Secrets to Success, Wealth, and Happiness* as creative persistence, a smart-working effort rightly planned and performed in a timely, efficient, and effective manner to attain a pure and high-quality result. When we display this attitude, success is not an option for the future, but an obtainable outcome.

6. Obedience is compliance with an order, request, or law, or submission to another's authority. It carries with it a social influence connotation that causes others to comply to a certain direction of vision and thought. Obedience leads to discipline, enabling us to reach our goals and attain various levels of success.

7. **Focus** is the quality of having or producing a clear, visual definition. An attitude of focus lets us clearly see the vision ahead in the midst of many other distractions that try to take our eyes off of what is important. We go where our focus goes. Focus requires us to stay on top of our crafts and keep striving to be better.

Developing confidence from self-development

An attitude of success breeds an Attitude of Confidence to discover and live your best life. Confidence is defined as an assurance, trust, or reliance on something or someone—including yourself.

When I first became chief executive officer at Ability Plus, it was failing financially. In addition, internal issues with staffing and leadership had taken their toll, and the people there had no confidence. I needed to trust that I was in that position at that particular time to do something different. Because of that conviction, I wasn't afraid of what would happen down the road, and when there were hard choices, we made them knowing that we would get back to a place higher than where we were before.

> Confidence is defined as an assurance, trust, or reliance on something or someone—including yourself.

That was exactly what happened. I had an opportunity to influence leaders, teammates, and younger professionals by looking at our company's culture. In a year-and-a-half, we dramatically turned around that culture, and the company's bottom line, through teaching and mentorship. I worked with the staff to change their behavior and outlook on what was possible, and that instilled confidence. I encouraged people to do their best and then asked the question, "Are you sure that is your best?" As a result, they went above and beyond, didn't complain, and became innovative within their own departments, doing things in a smarter and more consistent way.

Such confidence does not come automatically. Rather, confidence is an attribute that comes from our diligence reading, studying, and applying positive, self-help techniques such as those found in this book. Rem Jackson, founder and CEO of Top Practices, LLC, points out how people usually place a high value on education—up to a point. "However, many people stop actively seeking to learn, develop, and grow different areas of their lives and interests when they graduate and move into the workforce. The most successful businesspeople and medical professionals out there, however, never stop learning, and I don't just mean continuing education or studying for boards. Self-improvement and personal growth are an important, and highly valuable, part of your career and life in general."

He concludes, "Personal growth is a process of both understanding yourself and pushing yourself to reach your highest potential. It means always asking yourself who you are becoming and how you plan to get there. It can involve working on new habits and hobbies, fostering new skills, and practicing new strategies to achieve your goals. While this development starts very personal, it radiates outward and touches every aspect of your life, including your practice and professional growth."[12]

In my corporate presentation entitled "The Champion Mindset," I detail five mentalities that make a leader a champion. One of those is the willingness to learn—and I break that mentality down into three essential steps:

Gather ideas from a variety of sources. This speaks to the power of *thorough research*. As an engineer, I resonated with Lauren Landry's thoughts regarding the business skills every engineer needs. She wrote, "As technology continues to disrupt industries, the engineers who will advance are those who know how to spot emerging opportunities and validate their ideas. In an increasingly complex global business environment, companies can't keep approaching issues the same way. Engineers play a pivotal role in researching and identifying new business strategies."[13]

Strong researching abilities are best defined by following the scientific method, which is a tried-and-true systemic approach used to study and understand something by employing the following steps:[14]

1. Empirical observation: Objective observations using your senses or instruments to gather data.
2. Formulation of a hypothesis: A testable statement or prediction that proposes an explanation for a specific observation.
3. Testing and experimentation: Observational studies to test the validity of your hypothesis by gathering data to provide evidence for or against the hypothesis.
4. Data collection and analysis: Qualitative or quantitative data is then analyzed using statistical methods or other techniques to draw meaningful conclusions.
5. Reproducibility and verification: Others should be able to replicate the study and obtain similar results to validate the findings. One of the hallmarks of the scientific method is that experiments and observations should be reproducible.

6. Peer review: Research usually undergoes a peer review process where other subject matter experts evaluate your methodology, results, and conclusions to ensure the quality and credibility of your research.
7. Revision and refinement: The scientific method is an iterative process. New evidence or data may lead to the revision of hypotheses or theories. Therefore, your understanding of something evolves over time.
8. Objectivity and impartiality: Minimizing bias and personal beliefs that could influence your results is mandatory to research excellence.
9. Falsifiability: There should be the possibility of obtaining evidence that contradicts or refutes the proposed explanation. Research findings must be testable and falsifiable.

Ask yourself: What do I need to research and thoroughly test to better myself so I can grow personally and professionally?

Accurately evaluate a situation based on your knowledge of the situation. This speaks to the benefit of *informed discernment*. Once you have gathered your ideas, researched them, and thoroughly tested them, you need to apply them. Former president of Cornerstone University, Joseph Stowell, once said that discernment is the skill that "enables us to differentiate. It is the ability to see issues clearly … We must be prepared to distinguish light from darkness, truth from error, best from better, righteousness from unrighteousness, purity from defilement, and principles from pragmatics."[15]

Ask yourself: What do I need to apply from my research so that I will know how to better myself so I can grow personally and professionally?

Combine good ideas with the details of the situation to make changes in your behavior personally and organizationally. This speaks to the outcome of *proactive adaptability*. Issac Newton's First Law of Motion states, "Everything continues in a state of rest unless it is compelled to change by forces impressed upon it." Expert gardeners know that giving new bedding plants some rough treatment at planting time may be the best thing you can do to help them survive in the garden. If a plant has been growing in its pot so long that the roots are circling the bottom, don't hesitate to jab your finger into the bottom of the soil and pull down to untangle the roots. If you break some of the roots in the process, that's okay. It's far better than allowing the remaining roots to continue to circle when the plant is set into the garden soil.[16]

There's no need to be complacent and comfortable with where you are right now. The healthiest thing you can do is shake up your roots and plant them in new soil. Intentionally adapt and change your present state toward a wiser, more educated future state of self-development.

Ask yourself: Using what I have learned, what do I need to change to better myself so I can grow personally and professionally?

As you use information to change your situation, you will grow your confidence and elevate your attitude.

Signs of a lack of confidence

There are many signs that'll show up if we are not reflecting an Attitude of Confidence. Each one is like a road signal that warns us that we are about to take a wrong turn, and each one will hurt your quest to live your best life.

One sign is *frustration and anxiety*. Both indicate that we are upset about something that is not happening the way we thought it should. Yet we must constantly know and accept that such emotions only extract interest on trouble before it comes due. They constantly drain the energy you need to face daily problems and fulfill your many responsibilities. A woman who had lived long enough to have learned some important truths about life once remarked, "I've had a lot of trouble—most of which never happened!" She had allowed herself to become frustrated and anxious about many things that had never occurred, and she had come to see the total futility of her actions. An unknown poet wrote, "I heard a voice at evening softly say / Bear not your yesterdays into tomorrow / Nor load this week with last week's load of sorrow / Lift all your burdens as they come, nor try / To weigh the present with the by-and-by / One step and then another, take your way / Live day by day!"[17]

Another sign that we are not reflecting an Attitude of Confidence is *offensiveness*. Many times, offenses come up against us which are designed to knock down our confidence. They may come in the form of a lack of acknowledgment, a correction to a certain negative behavior, or an absence of support. When we allow these offenses to get the best of us, we must be careful not to stoop to their level in retaliation.

One of the rarest of management skills, and one of the most difficult to learn, is the ability to deal with criticism. Constructive criticism shows consideration for other people's feelings and invites their suggestions and cooperation. Criticism that starts out by attacking people and putting them in the position of having to defend themselves often turns small problems into big ones. Usually, the best way to start is with simple, friendly questions or queries that will give people a chance to explain their position without being offended and without getting excited.

Then, after you've listened carefully, suggest the changes you'd like them to make, whatever they are, and see what they think of them. Don't push for an immediate decision if it isn't necessary or if there is still substantial disagreement. Ask them to think it over. Tell them you will, too. Later, if you still believe in the changes you want to make, get together with them again. Explain that you've thought it over carefully and still believe the idea is worth a try. Tell them you feel an obligation to give it a fair chance, and you're counting on them to do the same.[18]

The next sign is *jealousy and envy*. There is no need to be jealous or envious of what someone has or something they have done. To envy is to want something which belongs to another person. In contrast, jealousy is the fear that something which we possess will be taken away by another person. Although jealousy can apply to our jobs, our possessions, or our reputations, the word more often refers to anxiety which comes when we are afraid that the affections of a loved one might be lost to a rival.[19] No matter what it is or who you are, there are opportunities for you to be a person of value and success regardless of what others have or want from you. Keep things in perspective. Someone once asked Paul Harvey, the beloved journalist and radio commentator, to reveal the secret of his success. He replied, "I get up when I fall down."[20]

The final sign that we are not reflecting an Attitude of Confidence is *feeling down on ourselves.* This happens when we do not work out, remove, and destroy the issues at the root of our feelings. We can live in victory and joy as we face our emotions

Attitude of Confidence

and problems with strength and courage. Author Leo Buscaglia told this story about his mother and their "misery dinner." It happened the night after his father came home and said it looked as if he would have to go into bankruptcy because his partner had absconded with their firm's funds. His father was discouraged, yet his mother went out and sold some jewelry to buy food for a sumptuous feast. When other members of the family scolded her for it, she told them that "the time for joy is now, when we need it most, not next week." Her act rallied his father and their entire family.[21]

In his autobiography, *Taken on Trust*, Terry Waite recounted his horrendous experience as a hostage in Beirut prisons for 1,763 days, almost four years of which were spent in solitary confinement. His first cell, underground, measured seven feet by 10 feet. The height varied between six and seven feet. Although living in such cramped quarters, Waite made himself walk. Some days he estimated he walked seven miles. Day and night were indistinguishable. He was led to the bathroom once each day.

Early in his detainment, Waite vowed that his captors would not capture his confidence. "Whatever is done to my body," he determined, "I will fight to the end to keep my inner freedom." He discovered that prayer and fasting increased his emotional strength. From memory, he recited the communion service regarded in the *Book of Common Prayer*.

A man who had once served as envoy for the Archbishop of Canterbury and had personally negotiated hostage releases had himself become the hostage—yet he accepted his situation and recited the mantra, "No regrets, no sentimentality, no self-pity."[22]

Terry Waite not only retained an Attitude of Confidence, he exercised incredible control of his emotions. Such emotional intelligence is vital to elevating your attitude, as you'll discover in the next chapter.

3
ATTITUDE OF EMOTIONAL INTELLIGENCE

Give thought and self-reflection to the emotional situations you encounter.

Many people get upset when pressures at work, frustrations at home, and other taxing life issues come upon them. When we don't have proper control over these situations, our attitude will reflect this through negative behavior.

According to Travis Bradberry, author of *Emotional Intelligence 2.0*, emotional intelligence is our ability to recognize and understand emotions in ourselves and others, and to use this awareness to manage our behavior and relationships. Daniel Goleman, regarded as the father of emotional intelligence (also known as emotional quotient or EQ), says EQ is managing feelings so that they are expressed appropriately and effectively, enabling people to work together smoothly toward their common goals. EQ expert Steve Hein defines emotional intelligence as the combination of innate emotional sensitivity with learned emotional management skills, which together lead to long-term happiness and survival.

When we first become aware of our own emotions and those of others, we can start to manage our attitude in such a way as to produce positive change and results. Therefore, to have self-control over our emotions, and the emotional reactions of others toward us, is an Attitude of Emotional Intelligence.

Our attitude is a product of our behavior and is based on our self-esteem, self-image, and self-efficacy (how well we respond to potential situations). We must monitor our Attitude of Emotional Intelligence daily to produce the positive mindset and behavior needed to get the desired results. It is very important that we continually work on managing what we feel and how our feelings affect others.

This is not something that just happens. We need to grow intentionally by placing our personal development on the forefront. We must give much thought and self-reflection to the emotional situations that we encounter every day. We can control our thoughts, and the attitudes that stem from them, when we understand them. I believe everyone wants to have the right attitude in times of peril, stress, and even triumph, but we often haven't developed the mindset to produce that attitude.

—*//*—

Emotional intelligence is commonly defined by five skills:

1. Self-awareness is the ability to recognize our own emotions and how they affect our thoughts and behavior. It also helps us to know our strengths and weaknesses, and to have self-confidence.

2. Self-management is the ability to understand changing situations and manage our feelings and behaviors in a healthy way. This produces a greater level of commitment and enables us to take on new and challenging things.

3. Social awareness is having empathy. This is the capacity to put ourselves in other people's shoes so we can feel their pain. We can do this by learning to understand their behavioral patterns, the differences in their personality types and temperaments, and being able to navigate through those differences.

4. Relationship management is the ability to influence other people to behave better and manage their own feelings. We do this by developing and maintaining good relationships, communicating clearly, inspiring others to work well in a team environment, and mediating conflict.

5. Self-motivation is a personal drive to improve and achieve, a commitment to goals and vision, and a desire to act on opportunities with optimism and resilience.

As we grow in these EQ skills, we will improve our mindset to produce an Attitude of Emotional Intelligence. Let's take a closer, personal look at each one of these skills from that perspective.

Skill 1: Self-awareness

You must know yourself. That knowledge arms you to manage yourself effectively. If you are a stranger to your emotions, fears, or even your purpose, you will live a strange life, one not meant for you, and you will be helpless to the waves of emotions that will drive your actions and decisions wherever they please. This will result in you depending on other people to define you, and you will be ruled by their opinions of you.

Yet I believe the power to define is the power to determine destiny. As a CEO, I constantly do self-reflections to better understand my emotions in critical situations. I don't act without first running my reactions through a series of filters. I ask myself questions such as, "Is this beneficial to me or the process?" "What does it take to get it done?" "Is this the proper time?" The answers to these questions slow me down just enough to process my emotions and think through the decision I am about to make. They ensure that I am not permitting my opinions to sway me or allowing a vibe that has no legitimacy to persuade me. I am able to get past *me* and get to the issue at hand.

> I believe the power to define is the power to determine destiny.

Skill 2: Self-management

Self-management is the ability to train your mind to strengthen and increase in capacity so that it is empowered to accept your feelings and maximize its energy to exhibit the right behavior, attitude, actions, and words. Your mind is like a knife. If you sharpen it, it cuts faster. If you don't, it becomes dull and inefficient.

Your mind is one of the greatest gifts you possess to help you live a successful life. But the imperfections associated with living dump a lot of junk into your mind. So, to get the best out of your mind, that junk has to be cleared out so your mind can be refurbished. A refurbished mind will help you maintain the right perception, and that's vital since you respond to issues based on what you perceive about them.

Through self-management, your mind is refurbished to allow its full potential to be reaped. Mind management takes care of personal and emotional management, and well managed emotions enable you to act, talk, and respond to issues in the right way, place, and time to the right people, as opposed to reacting to them. I'm quite intentional about managing my feelings and desires. There have been certain things that I felt like I needed right away, but I used the self-management strategy of delayed gratification to put them off for a more appropriate time. Delayed gratification is beneficial because it creates the time to build money, talent, or resources in order to obtain something. Then, when the opportune moment arrives, you'll have everything you need to be as productive and successful as possible.

I recall the time I had an opportunity to purchase another company. I really wanted it and would have bought it, but my self-management strategies helped me recognize that the purchase would've caused a major strain on the parent company. The company also had internal instability and some negative issues with client relations, so I decided it was best not to make the purchase. If I had not practiced delayed gratification, I may have jumped in with both feet and suffered severe consequences later.

Skill 3: Social awareness

Social awareness is a social skill that enables you to maintain harmony in your world through an existing inner peace. When you are able to understand other people's feelings and relate better to them, social awareness usually leads to positive action.

Result-oriented social awareness must be observant. You will need to study peoples' personality types to be able to understand their emotions. Through personality types, you will understand why others act, react, or talk a certain way. All three are the overflow of their emotional state. So, social awareness understands this and devises a means for you to manage them.

I have learned how to put myself in other people's shoes and try to understand their point of view. Once, one of our Ability Plus house managers came to me. He oversaw staff and programs for several of the homes we serve. He told me, "We need more funding because our responsibility is to fulfill what the budget demands." So, I shadowed him for a few days to assess his concern and find out what his days were like. In doing so, I discovered that while there were some capacity issues, we actually didn't need to put more resources into the homes to address those needs. In fact, we pulled back on some things so that the house manager could improve his planning and overall leadership. Shadowing him also made me more empathetic to the concerns he was dealing with, which he appreciated. It was helpful to everyone.

Skill 4: Relationship management

Relationship management is the ability to influence other people to behave better and manage their own feelings. Having good social skills and interpersonal relationships is a major facet of managing other people. You will always have to relate with other people. Learning this skill is vital in order to relate well with others in the workplace, at home, or in any group.

People have different temperaments, likes, and dislikes, and they bring different kinds of energy and understanding to situations. These differences will play out in the way they act, respond, or talk—so if you can manage those differences, you can maintain peace and maximize the benefits of those relationships.

I often teach others about their value and worth both to themselves and to their organizations. One time, I brought all of our mid-level managers together to participate in teamwork exercises designed to enhance our concern for one another and help overall production. These exercises focused on what they would do if they were in their peer's position in the company. They asked questions like, "What decisions would you make?" "How would you act?" We had role play sessions to help everyone appreciate what each person was doing and how each one brought value to the company. It built better relationships among the management team.

Skill 5: Self-motivation

Self-motivation is the ability to stir yourself to do what needs to be done without influence from other people. Another word for self-motivation is self-encouragement. Self-motivated people are enthusiastic. They have the ability to complete a task even in the face of barriers.

A crucial part of self-motivation is decision making. This can be daunting, and it can pull strongly on your emotions. Making hard decisions is not always easy, and it can be damaging if not properly handled. Every decision has consequences, and your decisions today will determine your quality of life tomorrow. Your decisions sculpt your destiny.

One of the things I do to motivate myself is to tell myself there are *no* bad days. I've chosen to never give in to disappointment and be sorry for an entire day. So, I gave each day a special name that I call, sign, and profess. For example, I call Sunday "Super Sunday." I sign it that day by using "Super Sunday" in my electronic messages. I profess it by saying "It's a Super Sunday" aloud throughout the day. I also came up with Marvelous

> **Your decisions sculpt your destiny.**

Monday, Terrific Tuesday, Wonderful Wednesday, Triumphant Thursday, Fantastic Friday, and Successful Saturday!

These started out as nothing more than titles, but I have since developed attributes, characteristics, and principles to go with each one, creating material to teach from these concepts. As a result, my self-motivation technique has become a powerful way to motivate others. One of my colleagues and a dear friend, Dr. Claudette Owens, attended a professional luncheon in 2022 where I was the keynote speaker. As told in her extraordinary book, *Recapturing Our Lost Identity: Overcoming the power brokers of greed and hate with the superpowers of love*, something amazing happened.

"As soon as I sat down," she wrote, "I could sense that something was going on inside the young lady to my right. Being able to feel what other people are feeling is nothing new to me. As I sat there next to this woman, that feeling became stronger and heavier ... Doc Rock was talking about not allowing yourself to have a bad day, but giving yourself a couple of moments, or a couple of hours at the most, to deal with negative or trying circumstances. He exhorted us that we should not allow those situations to control our entire day. Yet I could tell that the young lady next to me was troubled about something to the point that she was on the verge of giving up."

Claudette continued, "As Doc Rock instructed us to repeat the phrase, 'No bad days,' she looked at me and said, 'I'm trying.' Before I realized what I was doing, I reached for her hand, pulled her close to me, and spoke quietly into her ear. 'Life comes with uncertain blows. Some will even knock you down. That's okay. You have to get up, dust yourself off, and keep moving. The key to reaching our goals in life is to keep going in the right direction. Some days, you may move at a snails' pace;

others, you may move in sheer faith; and others still, you may move in pain. But the key is to keep moving. Moving is the only way you arrive at your destination. When you stop, you either enter a long layover or end up staying in a location you were never destined to be in. So, keep moving.' The smile that came to her face was priceless."

Claudette possessed the emotional intelligence to stir that woman to be self-motivated and find the inner strength to proceed.

As I stated earlier, an Attitude of Emotional Intelligence is not something that just happens. It has to be practiced daily and consistently.

BetterMe writer Clare Kamau's article, "Examples Of Emotional Intelligence To Practice In Daily Life," presented a scenario where someone in your life did something that you had already asked them not to do. She wrote that an emotionally intelligent person would:

- Recognize you are feeling angry that the other person disregarded your words and feelings.
- Realize that your anger makes you want to shout at or avoid the person, but that doesn't solve the situation. You may choose to walk away for the time being and perhaps journal or meditate to allow yourself to calm down.
- Once you've calmed down, you can approach the offending person, talk to them in private, and discuss the situation, expressing how the crossing of set boundaries made you feel. You can try to understand why the

person did it regardless of your opinion. You can also assert that it will not be allowed to happen again.
- Actively listen to the other person's explanation with an open heart and mind and try to understand the person's feelings and find common ground.[23]

I love that! Having and using emotional intelligence is all about elevating your attitude and applying your ability to recognize and understand emotions in yourself and others in each individual situation. Juanita Fourie, a creative writer in South Africa, posted on Quora two more practical stories of emotional intelligence in everyday life. She shared the following:

1. It is Saturday afternoon and, after having worked six consecutive days of 14 hours each, Michelle finally gets to leave the office.

    While stuck in traffic on her way home, the normally calm Michelle shouts a string of unsavory words at a group of cyclists snaking irresponsibly through the cars. On top of her boiling rage, she is suddenly reminded of her more-than-20-years-ago student days and the many lovely afternoons of cycling she and her first serious boyfriend enjoyed. Suddenly, she is overwhelmed by an intense feeling of nostalgia, which soon turns into great sadness that sees her breaking down into uncontrollable tears.

    "Don't worry, Michelle," she tells herself while taking a deep breath. "You are just tired and overemotional."

    Michelle understands her emotions and knows that they are coming from a place of lethargy following an unusually demanding workweek. She knows that a

long, hot bath and a good night's rest will see her back to her old self in no time.
2. Sam and his girlfriend just had a terrible fight. Knowing that getting out of the apartment would do him good, Sam decides to take a walk to the nearby park.

On his way there, he sees his nosy neighbor, Jim, along with Jim's irritating little mutt, walking toward him. Sam is most definitely not in the best of moods right now, and the last thing he needs is Jim's endless small talk and that ill-mannered mutt of his trying to pee on Sam's new Puma trainers.

As Jim and his fur ball approach, Sam takes a deep breath, calms himself, and greets his neighbor with a pleasant, "Hello, Jim!"

Sam thinks rationally about his anger and knows that it is not Jim's fault he is feeling this way. He knows that acting out toward his innocent neighbor would therefore be nothing short of unfair.[24]

As we develop new levels of mental and emotional self-management through an Attitude of Emotional Intelligence, we become more productive, more creative, and more responsive to the particular needs of others. For example, a positive organizational climate is created through leaders and team members who are internally aware of their emotions and those of others, and who are able to understand what is happening inside the organization with its business potential and people. Unless they create an environment that fosters mental and emotional balance by providing the information and motivation needed to help their people develop new self-management skills, organizations cannot expect to see long-term sustainable success in today's social and business world.

Of course, a reality that both individuals and companies deal with on an ongoing basis is money management. Our attitude toward money should be one of mission and purpose. Money is not just to spend, but to be a tool for life improvement—as we'll see next.

4
ATTITUDE OF MONEY

*Money is a resource,
not the source of your identity.*

The O'Jays sang about it back in the day: *Money, money, money, money—money!* They lamented of the drawbacks and hailed the benefits of the almighty dollar on society, and rightly concluded that "money can drive some people out of their minds!"

Everyone needs it, some want lots of it, and many love it, but far fewer people have a proper attitude about it. I totally believe that we can have millions, even billions, of dollars if we work hard for it—and the more money we have, the more we can do to help make a difference in this world.

I believe wealth and prosperity are blessings, but many people don't see or use their wealth that way because of their self-centered attitude toward money. We must learn to look at money—not as the source of who we are, but as a resource to get things done and make a positive difference.

What is money for?

Many people want to be rich, have plenty, and never have to rely on anything else. With all of their financial and material needs fulfilled, they'll never be in need, and therefore will never have to turn to anyone but themselves as their provider. Yet we must understand that even the millionaire must continue to go higher with his life's aspirations in order to experience true life fulfillment. Money exists so that we may use it wisely, not selfishly—and we are enabled to use money properly only because we have elevated our attitude about its use, misuse, and purpose.

Because of the systematic cycle we face each day, particularly in the workplace, it can be easy as employees or leaders to subconsciously begin placing our confidence in money, but we must avoid this tendency. Dr. I.V. Hilliard declared five things that should alert us that we have put too much trust in money.

> Money exists so that we may use it wisely, not selfishly.

1. When my worth and esteem is determined by what I possess. There was a young, up-and-coming man who believed that his importance came from the things he possessed. In fact, the more he bought, the better he felt about himself. He had a mentor who saw his potential and took the time to talk to him about developing a mindset of self-worth that was centered around principles of hard work and dedication. That attitude of self-esteem redefined how he thought about himself and brought new purpose to his life.

2. When a change in my financial state causes a change in how I treat others. After securing a promotion, a company leader began treating his fellow team members disrespectfully.

He looked down on everyone and didn't even acknowledge some of them. He made decisions without asking others on his team how they felt about it because he believed he was the big man in town.

Not until a true friend challenged his attitude of disrespect and taught him about servant leadership (see next chapter) did he realize that what he was doing was wrong. The leader was a smart guy who had great skills, but people follow others not because of their wits, charisma, or status, but because they trust and believe in that person. He developed an attitude where he put others first, and everything changed—including his misplaced confidence in money to define who he was and how he behaved.

3. When I begin to rationalize why I should not give what I should. There was a young lady who had been giving regularly to charitable organizations from her monthly pay. However, after a large sum of money was awarded to her, she decided that she had given enough and wanted to keep all of it for herself. She was challenged by her father, one of my colleagues, who reminded her that she'd been doing some good things and pointed her to principles that encouraged rather than corrected her. She chose to reinstate her practice of giving.

4. When I choose to violate proper principles of conduct to gain money. An organization that was doing well in its particular industry had an opportunity to gain more market share—but that chance was compromised when an annual audit of its operations and finances revealed some problems. The operations audit looked at what the organization did to ensure that it was following guidelines and principles for that industry, while the financial audit was designed to make sure the company's money was being allocated properly and that everything was on the straight and narrow taxwise. The organization's money was being so severely and fraudulently mismanaged that the CEO was fired, and new leadership was brought in to reinstate principles of responsibility and accountability.

5. When my financial state is valued above my integrity. When someone esteems what's in their pocketbook over their values, then their attitude about money is in error. Wanting to use money as a power source—to buy friendships or to maneuver and deceive people—instead of as a resource, reveals greed and self-centeredness.

The proper philosophy about money

You'll recall that philosophy is "loving the way we think," and we should love the way we perceive money. That includes understanding its potential pitfalls.

You've undoubtedly heard of "King Solomon's Mines." The subject of both popular literature and motion pictures, the monarch at the center of those stories is actually based on a real person from antiquity: the legendary biblical king renowned both for his wealth and his wisdom. A passage attributed to him in the Old Testament book of Ecclesiastes is entitled "The Foolishness of Riches," and it communicates one of Solomon's core philosophical conclusions about money and wealth.

"Whoever loves money never has enough; whoever loves wealth is never satisfied with their income. This too is meaningless. As goods increase, so do those who consume them. And what benefit are they to the owners except to feast their eyes on them? The sleep of a laborer is sweet, whether they eat little or much, but as for the rich, their abundance permits them no sleep."[25] Solomon believed monetary wealth could bring anxiety, so he finished that chapter by concluding that a person should find fulfillment in whatever lot he finds himself.

The foolishness of riches is quite real. Foolishness is defined as a lack of good judgment—and many people lack wisdom about the purpose of money. When we don't know the purpose of something, abuse is inevitable. We may spend all we gain for personal pleasure rather than engaging in delayed gratification, which is an essential practice to being a good steward that brings stability and prosperity in the long run. I knew a couple who received a large tax refund. Instead of saving some, or most, of that money to pay off bills and investing a portion of it, they spent all of it on household improvements. That choice wasn't bad in and of itself, but if they had better discerned how to use the refund, perhaps they could've reduced their debt while making some minor improvements on their home.

> When we don't know the purpose of something, abuse is inevitable.

While nice houses, automobiles, jewelry, or fancy clothing have their place for enjoyment in our lives, feeding the hungry, clothing the naked, and providing shelter for those who have no place to sleep is of far more value to others. So is providing education for those less fortunate than ourselves, giving them an opportunity to be in an environment geared for success.

Money is needed to achieve all of these needs—and each one allows you to use it as a resource to make your world a better place. There is a great organization I have worked with over the years in Honduras that builds schools, feeds the poor, and trains individuals to make a productive living. I made several trips to Honduras with this organization, doing everything from field work to leadership training. In addition, a company in our area that does work for the Department of Defense won a significant contract which considerably increased their revenue. It donated over $100,000 of that increase to an area non-profit organization that takes care of orphans.

Money is never just for you.

Maximizing money for yourself and others

A sage proverb states, "The wise person saves for the future, but the foolish person spends whatever they get." When it comes to money, the way to be wise is to be a saver. Four simple rules given by the late financier, J.P. Morgan, for saving money are a) start early. Today is the day to start your savings program; b) save a definite amount; c) save regularly and systematically; and d) employ your savings productively.[26]

Another wise but often underutilized key to wise money management is minimizing or eliminating debt, particularly consumer debt. One person quipped, "The only reason a great many American families don't own an elephant is that they have never been offered an elephant for a dollar down and easy weekly payments."[27] Seriously, the accumulation of personal financial debt has resulted in many families suffering hardship including loss of their homes and even bankruptcy. Debt has contributed to fractured or ended relationships. Buying and accumulating things, even if they are legitimate needs, with credit (money you really don't have) is a foolish pitfall best to avoid.

Finally, a sound money management strategy is to utilize portions of your income or savings to create more money. In her book, *The Nuts and Bolts of Investing*, investment and securities advisor Carol Jones offered basic facts to both novice and seasoned investors to help them make good decisions with their money. When it came to handling money and investments, Carol saw the process as being much like a journey.

"Normally, you begin with a destination in mind, and then make a plan about how to get there ... You really can't begin unless you've set some goals and then developed a plan. Without this preparation, you might take profits or losses at the wrong times, lose track of your portfolio, or buy an inappropriate investment on the spur of the moment. Once you figure out your goals to clarify your investment objectives, you can then work your plan with the knowledge of how much money you have, what you want to put that money into, and why you are doing it."

As you consider how you can elevate your attitude by maximizing the money you have now, and will earn in the future, as a resource for yourself and a benefit to others, here is a collection of practical facts and tips from Carol's book.

1. Before investing, your current income must cover your basic living expenses, plus emergencies such as a broken furnace or car repairs. You must also have adequate insurance.
2. Begin your investment journey by putting the maximum dollars allowed into a retirement savings plan. After that, you use whatever is left to build an investment portfolio.
3. Shares of *stock* represent ownership capital in a corporation and are usually bought in 100-share lots (a standard number of trading units), although it is possible to buy as little as a single share of a stock.
4. A *bond* is a fixed income investment in which you loan money to an entity for a defined period of time

at a variable or fixed interest rate. Bonds are generally purchased in one- to five-thousand-dollar blocks.
5. Most *mutual funds*, holding companies where shareholder's funds are pooled and invested by a money manager, require much smaller minimum purchases; some will take as little as twenty-five dollars. Regular, small investments in a mutual fund may be a great way to start investing while minimizing risk. You simply want to make sure that the costs you pay your broker or investment advisor for small purchases are reasonable.
6. Investment *risk* refers to the likelihood that you will lose your money in that investment. Have a clear understanding of the risk involved before you make any investment decision. Investments whose values do not fluctuate carry the lowest degree of risk, but historically have the lowest rate of return over long periods of time. Other investments may be subject to large fluctuations in value. They come with a higher degree of risk of losing your money, but also have the chance to realize the highest returns.

Balancing risk and return is an essential part of building a portfolio. In general, a younger person with good earning power and some savings has time to weather riskier investments, while someone past retirement age usually cannot replace large financial losses and would be better served by conservative investments.

Here are some questions you'll need to ponder before you decide what kinds of investments to make:
1. What standard of living do you have now?

2. Do you want it to continue, and for how long?
3. What are your retirement goals?
4. Do you have children to educate or aging parents to support?
5. What kind of financial risks are you willing to take?
6. How much time do you have for your investments to produce the results you want, especially before you retire?

Once you've answered these questions, you can determine where to allocate your investment dollars and perhaps discuss these questions with a certified financial planner.[28]

Remember, money is a resource—so while your finances should never be the source of your identity, it can certainly be an *extension* of your identity, shown in your mindset about how you use it. In *Financial Healing from the Inside Out*, my longtime colleague, Dr. Amanda H. Goodson, and her co-author, Angela C. Preston, cite the importance of having a healthy relationship with money. "Virtually every major decision you make involves some consideration of the monetary consequences," they wrote. "What you do, where you live, and with whom you associate are all impacted by your mindset about money. Often, those attitudes and beliefs come from your childhood or cultural experiences that taint your perspective. Examining the source of our mindset allows you to discard thinking that no longer serves your purpose, allowing you to create a new set of attitudes and beliefs."

When you have the right attitude about money, the result is freedom. Goodson and Preston say it best. "Financial freedom may look different for each person, but freedom from finances generally means being free of all debt: no outstanding loans, no credit card debt (never carrying any balances forward and incurring added interest), and no mortgages. It means no payments to anyone for any reason. Financial freedom can also mean that you now have multiple revenue streams—savings and investments that allow enough flexibility for you to be able to retire to do what you want when you want and how often you want, where you choose to do it for however long you want to do it. Financial freedom is being able to enjoy a self-directed life where you get to call all the shots in terms of how, when, and where you spend your time. Financial freedom may also be the choice of living a frugal lifestyle rather than acting in an irresponsible manner, especially if failure to do so will put your financial freedom at risk."

They conclude, "True financial freedom shows that you have taken control of your finances."[29]

—#—

As we elevate our attitudes about our confidence, emotional intelligence, and money, we are then positioned to be leaders in our society, our workplaces, and our homes.

It is an incredible responsibility, and our success is predicated on following the right example.

5
ATTITUDE OF A SUCCESSFUL LEADER

Look out for other people and put them first.

In his book, *The Spirit of Leadership: Cultivating the Attributes That Influence Human Action*, leadership consultant Dr. Myles Munroe defined leadership as "the capacity to influence others through inspiration, motivated by a passion, generated by a vision, produced by a conviction, and ignited by a purpose." Leadership expert John C. Maxwell simply said, "leadership is influence, nothing more, nothing less."

When the board of directors of a large food company was considering the selection of a new president, one of the directors worked out this questionnaire. Read each question slowly and carefully. Every one of them is telling when it comes to the qualities of a successful leader who looks out for others and puts them first.

1. Who of the possible candidates is the best known as a personality to the most company people?

2. Who is the most liked and trusted by them?
3. Who is held in the highest regard outside the organization...in public life and in the trade?
4. Who is the most warmly human when dealing with people?
5. Who has demonstrated the best capacity for selecting able people and the greatest willingness to delegate authority and responsibility?
6. Who will be apt to do the best job of keeping his or her desk and mind clear of day-to-day operating problems in order to have time to think in broader terms of tomorrow and next year?
7. Who does the boldest—yet soundest—thinking?
8. Who is most open-minded and willing to revise decisions when important new facts come to light?
9. Who inspires the best cooperation and exercises the best control and coordination without trespassing on responsibility once delegated?
10. Who is most self-possessed in all situations, best able to adjust to personalities and circumstances with tact and understanding?
11. Who can be depended upon to make the most of a promising new plan or idea?
12. Who can "take it" the best under a heavy load of responsibility?
13. Who is the best builder of the people?
14. Who is most likely, in good times and bad, to remember that the basic job of the president is to operate the business at a profit?[30]

Helping others win

Mark Miller, the vice president of High Performance Leadership at Chick-Fil-A, elaborated on servant leadership in his book, *The Heart of Leadership: Becoming a Leader People Want to Follow*. He wrote, "Servant leadership is an approach contrary to conventional leadership in which the leader's focus is on himself and what he can accomplish and achieve. Rather, the focus is on those being served." While Miller said servant leaders do many of the same things other leaders do, such as cast vision and build teams, the big difference is their orientation and motivation. "They possess an others-first mindset. The servant leader constantly works to help others win."

I once hired a female leader who had a lot of potential to be a great executive. She possessed talent in decision making, change management, and team building. She had a big drive for excellence. She wanted to be the best and to help as much as possible, and she was on board with the vision that I had cast for the company. Her ceiling of advancement was high, so I set aside time to become a mentor to her. We discussed improvement in areas such as people skills and in having overall wisdom when making executive decisions. The time I dedicated to her was taken from time that I could have been doing things for myself, but I decided to put her future first. She was a very open-minded mentee who took to heart everything she learned. Within three years, she had advanced in her career and currently serves as our vice president of operations.

Servant leadership also works because it honors others— acknowledging their different roles, responsibilities, and strengths. As Miller put it, "It is not about who's in charge. It's about who is responsible for what, and how can I, as the leader, help people be successful."

A super guy who possessed the rare talents of negotiation and conflict resolution came into my circle when we sat on the same non-profit board. Immediately recognizing his gifting, I hired him to fulfill a few specific roles to help take my organization to another level, first as a consultant and later as a staff member. I acknowledged his strengths and put them to use in various ways—and he told me it was his confidence in my leadership philosophy that helped him to grow and be able to improve those around him. In that philosophy, I allow people to fail and learn from their mistakes, all while knowing that I have their backs. It was something he had never seen in other leaders, and it allowed him to have a safe place to mature and allow his talents to flourish. It continues to be a joy to watch him work and grow.

> Servant leadership works because it honors others.

Leaders who are servants don't blame others. They own their actions and their outcomes. This speaks to accountability where leaders praise others on their team when they do well and take full responsibility for the good or bad outcomes of the team. Ability Plus is an organization with many moving parts that is monitored by strict state rules. We are subject to an annual audit from the state that requires us to accept auditors who have different personalities and want things done in various formats. Therefore, we often have to go to our house managers and other staff during the audit period with demands that can bring great stress to our entire team.

In 2021, during our annual review from the state regarding the services we provide, we were cited in several areas, and the auditor went over all the improvements needed for our organization to be in full compliance. Instead of blaming my team for the problems at hand, I told the auditors that the issues were my responsibility as CEO and that we would address them and move to a positive status. I promised to personally oversee the process to the end. It's difficult to take responsibility instead of passing it on to others, but it's always best to be proactive rather than reactive. I asked myself, "What did I do to help them get their job done?" "Did I do everything I could to help them?" "Was I as fully supportive as I needed to be?" This type of accountability helps me to get better and to know the strengths and weaknesses of those who follow me on my team.

Finally, servant leaders are men and women who see things *that could be*—and Miller pointed out that the future they see is always a better version of the present. "We believe we can make a difference; we think we can make the world, or at least our part of it, better," he said. When I took over Ability Plus, the company was in big trouble from a financial, structural, and cultural viewpoint. As a servant leader, I addressed the team to let them know that we were going to be better in the future. I did not have all the answers or the resources, but I had the mindset to roll up my sleeves and get to work with a determination to motivate others to do the same. I told the staff that I would not ask them to do anything that I wasn't willing to do myself. They saw me get up every day and stay in the fight with them. I told them often that I appreciated what they did. I told them we would learn as we went. We all leaned on each other's strengths—and we turned things around.

Foundational attitudes of great leadership

Leaders think differently about themselves. That is what distinguishes them from followers. I've identified seven attitudes that are foundational to great leadership. Some of these attitudes may be more present in the personality of one leader than another, but each of these attitudes can be strengthened. Whether they naturally possess these qualities or not, great leaders are diligent to consistently develop each one of these attitudes to elevate their unique leadership roles.

1. A great leader has exemplary character

Miller wrote of leadership being like an iceberg: 10 percent above the waterline and about 90 percent below. The part above the water indicates leadership skills, but the rest below represents leadership character. "If you want to predict people's ultimate success as leaders," Miller said, "evaluate not their skills but their leadership character."

It is of utmost importance that leaders are trustworthy. They should be known to live with honesty and integrity. Great leaders "walk the talk," earning the right to have responsibility for others as they do. Servant leadership builds trust simply because we trust leaders whose motives are centered around others.

In an interview with Women.com, actress Jodie Foster was asked about corporate leadership success, and her answer likely surprised a few readers.

Women.com: Back to the topic of leadership, what else can we be doing to promote leadership in women?

Foster: Well, I have this really outdated philosophy about success in a corporate structure, and you're going to think I'm really romantic and a fool, but here it goes. I think that if you are moral and you're right and you have the right ethics, that eventually somewhere down the line you're going to end up being successful.

In our business, anyway, you're always going up and down, and at some point you're going to find yourself down. You're going to need somebody to say, "Hey, I remember you. You're the one that treated me right, and I'm going to lend a hand out to you." It's your responsibility to conduct yourself ethically throughout the process—always ethics first—so that somewhere down the line, somebody's going to let you live up to your own potential.

Women.com: Do you live your life that way as well?

Foster: Yeah, I really do. I mean, I think I try to be the best person I can. Lord knows I make big mistakes. I make big mistakes all the time. But I try to be as honest and direct as I can.[31]

True authority is born out of the respect and trustworthiness shown by great leaders. In addition, servant leaders should be people of fiscal responsibility and, when needed, monetary sacrifice. While working as CEO of Ability Plus, I received an offer to take a job that would've tripled my annual salary and provided other attractive benefits. It was an incredible opportunity, but after prayer and counsel from other trusted people, I decided that purpose, not money, should be the criteria to take the position. When we chase our purpose and passion, money will follow. Money is not the endgame. I turned down the offer to remain in my purpose and passion at Ability Plus, knowing that when you walk in your purpose, you are walking in you.

2. A great leader is enthusiastic about their work or cause as well as about their role as a leader

It's undeniable that people will respond more openly to a person of passion and dedication. Leaders need to be a source of inspiration and a motivator toward the required action or cause. Although the responsibilities and roles of each one of these leaders may be different, they need to be part of the team, unafraid to roll up their sleeves and get dirty. Tom Landry, former head coach of the National Football League's Dallas Cowboys and one of the finest leaders professional sports has ever known, once said, "Leadership is a matter of having people look at you and gain confidence, seeing how you react."[32]

Early in my career as a pastor, my first church was a young ministry that was growing at a constant rate. That meant our initial facility was not sufficient for us to have the programs and outreaches we wanted for the community. So, I found an old warehouse that had a lot of potential but was quite run down. It needed a ton of work, but I was enthusiastic about what we could do with the building.

As an engineer, I mentally drew up my plans for it and communicated them to my church leadership team. We got the property, remodeled it, and used it for the next three years. The highlight was the summer youth program that it allowed us to facilitate. After moving into the building, one of my elders revealed that, in reality, the leadership team didn't see anything that I saw in my mind, but my enthusiasm caused them to follow my recommendation to acquire the building.

3. A great leader is confident

In order to set direction, leaders need to be confident as individuals and in their leadership role. Such a person inspires confidence in others and draws out the trust of the team to complete the task well. A leader who conveys confidence toward the proposed objective brings out the best in all those around them. Dr. John Haggai, the great outreach executive who raised up leaders worldwide, once said, "Leadership is the discipline of deliberately exerting special influence within a group to move it towards goals of beneficial permanence that fulfills the group's real needs."[33]

When I started doing leadership consulting through Vision Excellence Company, I didn't know anyone who had started such a company. Yet I had a vision in my heart for it. Within three months of moving forward, two doors of opportunity opened up to consult with two different organizations. I didn't have all the know-how I needed, but I did know that I would succeed. I was confident in myself and my vision. That humble beginning has developed into a team providing seminars, training, and coaching in a dozen different strategic areas to help individuals and organizations lead, innovate, and grow.

4. A great leader functions in an orderly and purposeful manner during times of uncertainty

People look to their leaders during transition or turmoil. During the Nazi occupation of his country in World War II, King Christian X of Denmark noticed a Nazi flag flying over a Danish public building. He immediately called the German commandant, demanding that the flag be taken down at once. The commandant refused.

"Then a soldier will go and take it down." said the king.
"He will be shot," threatened the commandant.
"I think not," replied the king, "for I shall be the soldier."
Within minutes, the flag was taken down.[34]

Others find reassurance and security when their leaders portray a positive demeanor in trial or difficulty. As a member of the advisory board for the business school at Alabama A&M University, I was tasked with serving on a committee to assist the dean, faculty, and staff to achieve international accreditation. There were many requirements to get the certification, and we could not be distracted with others' opinions about how hard it was going to be to achieve that status. The dean was a fearless leader who kept every meeting and work session in line with order and purpose. He made sure everyone knew before each meeting what was going to be talked about, and he provided the background information we needed so we would be prepared to discuss next steps to achieve the accreditation.

It took two years, but we got it done. That international accreditation serves to protect the interests of the university's students, their parents, the institution, and potential employers by ensuring that the educational programs offered have attained a level that meets or exceeds standards that were developed by experts in their fields.

5. A great leader is tolerant of ambiguity and remains calm, composed, and steadfast to the main purpose

Storms, emotions, and crises come and go—and great leaders take these as part of the journey and keeps a cool head in the midst of them. It's been said that the first responsibility of a leader is to define reality. Leaders need to have a good picture of what is really going on around them, and they need to help others take an honest look at this reality.[35]

During the 2021 audit of Ability Plus that I mentioned earlier, the state representative asked to see our procedures for tracking the behaviors of our clients. These behaviors can include acting out, a response to a medical treatment, or a deterioration in their overall condition. We had recorded this information using a form the state representative didn't like or understand—so we had no other choice than to change our form and tracking procedures to fit the representative's request. We had to take the information we had, put it into the new form, and then make sure the procedures read the way the state wanted. This took weeks, and to say the least, was not appealing to our team. But we reminded one another to stay calm under pressure.

6. A great leader is able to think analytically and stay focused on the goal

Not only do great leaders view a situation as a whole, but they are able to break it down into subparts for closer inspection. Not only is the end goal in view, but it can be broken down into manageable steps so that progress can be made. Leadership is the ability to put the plans into practice, and to accomplish the specified objectives through the skillful management of people, time, and tangible resources. A good leader is one who is able to motivate people; one who is capable of making good decisions, even under pressure or in conditions of uncertainty; one who can guide people through actions as well as words.[36]

When I launched Vision Excellence Company, I had a goal of becoming more involved in the community because I wanted to increase my influence among senior leaders in northern Alabama. After receiving advice on how to proceed with this goal, I developed a plan to achieve it that focused on leading with purpose and making a difference in the community. It couldn't be done all at once, so I had to exercise patience along the way as each step required a different level of maturity.

First, I established a relationship and partnership with the local Chamber of Commerce. Second, I started to support community charities by attending several of their monthly and annual events. Third, I served on the boards of six different non-profit organizations in the region. This led to me being asked to be part of several key groups of influence, helping me to learn and grow from other leaders throughout the area. I was allowed to offer my advice and guidance to address issues from workforce development and diversity and inclusion matters to annual fundraising campaigns and providing leader mentorship. In all, it took four years to achieve my goal, and I not only met my expectations, but I exceeded them.

7. A great leader is committed to excellence

Second best does not lead to success. Great leaders not only maintain high standards, but they are proactive in raising the bar in order to achieve excellence in all areas. Someone once said, "Do not follow where the path may lead, go instead where there is no path and leave a trail."[37]

When the COVID-19 pandemic hit our world in 2020, many companies and organizations had to start operating in different ways. This included doing more with technology and media. At my church, we had to turn to live streaming as the main source of programming to our members. We had already been doing a live stream, but it was only as a second option to in-person attendance and participation. We realized we had to deliver a better and improved virtual experience as the pandemic kept most people at home.

> Second best does not lead to success.

I got our leadership together with our IT and media team to create a plan to produce a live streaming broadcast of excellence. This required all of us working together not just on technical changes, but also on how we conducted our services. Everyone got on board, and the response was overwhelmingly positive. Workers, volunteers, and congregants had an attitude of success. Those watching the stream liked the upgraded cameras and the new backdrop. This commitment to excellence caused everyone to look at what they were doing and ask how they could do it better.

"In order to be a leader, a man must have followers—and to have followers, a man must have their confidence. Hence the supreme quality of a leader is unquestionably integrity. Without it, no real success is possible, no matter whether it is on a section gang, on a football field, in an army, or in an office. If a man's associates find him guilty of phoniness, if they find that he lacks forthright integrity, he will fail. His teachings and actions must square with each other. The first great need, therefore, is integrity and high purpose."[38]

That quote, spoken by President Dwight D. Eisenhower, rings true for leaders of all genders and from all walks of life. All of us need to be successful leaders—and that elevated attitude requires us to look out for other people and put them first. In order to put others first, we need to be part of a team. Each one of us accomplishes more when we're in it together.

No leader does anything on their own. They don't take credit on their own. They don't turn the company around on their own. They don't make progress on their own. It takes a team with everybody doing their part and operating in their expertise—and that's what we'll talk about next.

6
ATTITUDE OF TEAMWORK

*All devoted to one. One devoted to all.
That is what makes up an effective team.*

I first learned how to build an effective cohesive leadership team not in business, but as a pastor. When my wife and I launched Emmanuel The Connection Church in 1996, we immediately recognized that we needed a team to succeed in our vision of saving and empowering people. The mission was too big for a couple of people to achieve. More than that, we did not want to be just another building on the corner with a name on it. We wanted our church to make a real difference in the Huntsville community.

We had all these ideas of what we wanted to do, but we had to plan, discuss, and agree upon who was going to do what, when they were going to do it, and how they were going to get it done. We had to be on the same page. It was a challenge because we had some people who had left other church organizations to be a part of ours, and each one came to us with different titles, roles, and abilities. We had to help them understand our vision and how they fit into making it come to pass.

We started by teaching the team about talents to find out their strengths. Next, we laid out the specific outreaches we wanted to do, and we assessed where everyone fit best. We took it one step at a time and asked everybody to be a team player.

It took a year-and-a-half to get where we needed to be, but we did it—and our church indeed had a phenomenal impact in the community because we worked as a team.

Essential elements of teamwork

Bees teach us something about teamwork. On a warm day about half the bees in a hive stay inside beating their wings while the other half go out to gather pollen and nectar. Because of the beating wings, the temperature inside the hive is about 10 degrees cooler than outside. The bees rotate duties and the bees that cool the hive one day are honey gatherers the next.[39]

Bear Bryant, the legendary University of Alabama football coach, said this about developing a winning team. "I'm just a plow hand from Arkansas, but I have learned how to hold a team together. How to lift some men up, how to calm down others, until finally they've got one heartbeat together, a team. There's just three things I'd ever say: If anything goes bad, I did it. If anything goes semi-good, then we did it. If anything goes real good, then you did it. That's all it takes to get people to win football games for you."[40]

In whatever setting you operate, there is no substitute for having an Attitude of Teamwork. First, **support of one another** is critical in teamwork. The entire group of people who make up the team are not supported by one person, but by each other. They are stronger together operating on the same plan. Teamwork is the key to achieving our dreams and, from an organizational perspective, to accomplishing our mission and vision.

Second, it is very important that each person on the team **knows their role.** Just as the many cultures of the world have their great followers and leaders, each team has great players, some who are destined to succeed individually, and others who are purposed to be leaders and will take their team to higher places. Whatever their role, each member of the team relies on the other. In a Peanuts cartoon, Lucy demanded that Linus change television channels, threatening him with her fist if he didn't. "What makes you think you can walk right in here and take over?" asked Linus.

"These five fingers," Lucy said. "Individually, they're nothing, but when I curl them together like this into a single unit, they form a weapon that is terrible to behold."

"Which channel do you want?" asks Linus. Then, turning away, he looked at his fingers and said, "Why can't you guys get organized like that?"[41]

Unity is the last essential element of teamwork. Unity is the glue that keeps everyone moving in the same direction for a common cause. Without unity, talents will find themselves in an unproductive state. "Snowflakes are one of nature's most fragile things," someone once said, "but just look at what they can do when they stick together."[42]

The biggest challenge to unity is making sure each person understands their goals and their roles in achieving those goals, then ensuring that every team member puts aside their individual egos. It is not about how I want to do it. It is about what needs to be done for the goal to be achieved. Many times, people have their own unique takes on how to get there, but there is a right way defined by our organizational values and culture. Recognizing individuality and talents to maximize them, then translating them in the team to the mission and purpose, is the key. They have to see how their individual goals are wrapped up in the overall goal so they can still achieve what they want, but to the benefit of the entire team.

In the end, no organization can be healthy without unity. I know that's a bold statement, but it is made after years of experience. When unification is absent in a team, individual gifts, talents and egos begin to war against each other. The project, process, and plans are ultimately destroyed, and the organization dies. I recall a statewide alliance of leaders that wanted to share in community projects and meet the needs of those less fortunate. But because of their lack of unity from a structural and organizational position, they failed, even after several attempts at trying to right the ship. They couldn't decide who was going to lead, and they did not have a clear mission or vision statement. In addition, they never pinpointed their overall "why." They knew they needed to exist, but they never got to their purpose.

> No organization can be healthy without unity.

On the other hand, there was an organization in Georgia that brought leaders together for training, empowerment, and collaboration, and it thrived. Each year, additional leaders from around the country joined their effort, and they had a positive impact on thousands of people. In their case, the leader had a clear vision and mission, precise objectives that he wanted to achieve, and everybody got on board. There was uncompromising unity, and that unity prompted growth and results.

Organizational effectiveness = team cohesiveness

The word "team" is often overused in the sense that we usually refer to any group with more than one person as a team. But a true team is not just two or more people, but a group that is moving in the same direction to accomplish a goal or mission. This necessitates cohesiveness—and there are three ways, when evaluating an organization, that team cohesiveness will bring about overall effectiveness.

1. Building the team. An organization needs a team that works well together. Functional, cross-functional, and self-managing teams are the three different types of teams found within an organization, and each team has its own specific goals and objectives. Functional teams are the traditional teams that generally have a lot of oversight and are in the same discipline: they are all engineers or accountants. Cross-functional teams have members from several disciplines, possibly including someone from marketing or human resources, working to achieve a particular goal. Self-managing teams come up with new ideas on their own. Management has approved this team's work in advance, and its members are not afraid to explore, act, and then present their results to executive leadership.

By resolving conflicts, brainstorming new solutions, initializing innovation, and providing a supportive and encouraging environment for all of these teams, you will improve the performance of individual team members and the organization as a whole. One of the greatest ways to do this is through team building activities. As you provide ample opportunities for the members of your team to interact with and get to know one another, they learn to trust and depend on each other and care for one another. Outdoor physical activities such as a Ropes Course or other obstacle courses are fun ways to learn to work together.

I also recommend seminars where team role playing exercises are used to hone communication and collaboration skills.

2. Establishing a goal pyramid. To create an efficient system for achieving goals and making viable progress in a timely manner, do what ancient architects did: create an unshakable structure with at least three levels—company goals, team goals, and individual goals. This goal pyramid starts with your ultimate vision at the very top, followed by team goals at the middle level, and individual tasks and objectives on the bottom. It is a fantastic tool to foster unity, provide transparency, and keep your employees from getting sidetracked from the predetermined road to success. Setting clear objectives on each level is a phenomenal way to measure progress, keep the operation's big-picture goals at the forefront of everyone's minds, and map out a way for every team member to contribute to the larger vision of the organization.

The goal pyramid is created with the executive team looking at the vision and mission statement from one-year, five-year, and 10-year perspectives, and then building company goals for each team and drilling down to establish team goals and what each person needs to do to accomplish those goals. The pyramid is first presented to the team in a group "lunch and learn" setting where they can get fired up, excited, and motivated. It is then shared in detail with team leaders and, through them, to each individual. This is exactly the type of work we do with our clients through Vision Excellence Company.

3. Fostering transparency. There is no better way to accomplish flawless team cohesion than by leading your crew with complete transparency. Business management expert and author Patrick Lencioni refers to this as "getting naked" in his book about client loyalty. It is vital to take the time to enlighten every member on goals, procedures, and policies while setting crystal clear objectives so that each member knows how they are expected to contribute to the overall success of the company. Leading with complete transparency provides everyone with a clear understanding of what they're working toward and how they can support the greater good of the organization. Never punish anyone for being transparent. In fact, you want to provide tips and guidance to encourage transparency and reward people for being transparent.

Integrity is required to establish and solidify transparency. Lencioni wrote that integrity is healthy when it is whole, consistent, and complete—meaning that operations, strategy, and culture all fit together and make sense. I've discovered that integrity can be further defined as the state of being honest and undivided. When operations are doing things in an honest way to support the overall strategic plan that encompasses the established culture, organizational health is achieved. Transparency mandates telling the truth, even if it hurts or costs you something. When you start compromising and not telling the truth, it becomes easier to do, and it infects the culture. Owning up to mistakes might be tough, but it is always the right thing to do.

Five key behaviors of effective teamwork

A *Chicago Tribune* article once told the story of Chad Kreuter, a reserve catcher for the Chicago White Sox, who severely dislocated and fractured his left shoulder on a play at home plate. He underwent surgery, and the White Sox placed him on the 60-day disabled list. That's exactly the kind of thing that can make a backup player feel even less like a part of the team.

But quite the opposite happened. Chad's teammates had a strong liking for him, so each one put Chad's uniform number 12 on his ball cap to show support. This gesture made Chad feel like he was a part of the team even though he couldn't play. Later in the season, after Chad was recovered and able to play once again, he showed his appreciation by putting the uniform number of each of his teammates, every one of them, on his cap.[43]

All devoted to one. One devoted to all. That is what makes up an effective team—and that type of devotion to one another is created and nurtured by five key behaviors.

1. Building trust. Dictionary.com defines a steward as someone who manages another's property or financial affairs; one who administers anything as the agent of another or others. Implicit with their role is that they can be fully trusted. In a business setting, a steward is defined as someone who uses resources in a systematic, accountable way and is concerned about the sustainability of the organization. This steward manages cash flow, employee relations, innovation, and other parts of the business for the betterment of the organization, its employees and customers, and any other stakeholders.

Successful stewardship begins by building trust within your team. There are two types of trust. Predictive trust involves knowing how someone on your team will react in a given situation. For example, my consulting firm worked for an insurance company that had an agent who was directed to build positive relationships and interactions with customers who had strong issues and concerns regarding their policies. We predicted that the agent would lose his cool when the customer pushed hard against him—and we were right. He was placed in a coaching program to train him on how to better work with people. He corrected his behavior, improved, and has done well ever since.

Then there is vulnerability-based trust where team members are completely transparent and honest with one another. When teams have this kind of trust, teammates can genuinely say to each other, "I need help," "I messed up," "I can learn from you," or "You are better at that." While working with a government contracting company and conducting Emotional Intelligence training with its staff, it was revealed that people there felt very safe to share their vulnerabilities with their teammates. They were not afraid of being disrespected or marginalized when asking for help or admitting that they had a problem. In the midst of the training, many others around the table started talking about when they had issues, and their teammates and leaders were very receptive. Everyone was on the same page, and there was clear camaraderie in place that improved the culture.

Of course, at the heart of vulnerability is a willingness to abandon self-pride and fear and sacrifice ego for the good of the team. There was a time when I was working with a large nonprofit organization where the executive director showed great vulnerability-based trust. The organization needed a change in culture and mindset to go to the next level, and he had to move past his ego and admit that how he had been leading the organization was not effective. He admitted to being a little off-center when it came to his vision for the future and where the industry was headed. He showed greater care for the business than for his pride, and he allowed others to help him correct his errors and create the culture change.

The main thing that prevents new team members from building trust is the Fundamental Attribution Error. First identified by social psychologist Lee Ross in 1977, this error speaks to our tendency as human beings to attribute the negative or frustrating behaviors of our colleagues to their intentions and personalities while attributing our own negative or frustrating behaviors to environmental factors.

I saw this happen one time when a mid-level manager at a particular company exhibited very negative behaviors that were consistently witnessed by her teammates and other peers. The manager was judgmental toward others in the company, even those outside of her department. She took punitive actions when she felt the behavior of others was not in sync with company policies or culture. She made statements that suggested others behaved in a way intended to harm or even destroy the company. Yet when this manager was confronted about her own behaviors, she always attributed them to the systems and conditions she was placed in by management. It wasn't until she received coaching that she recognized what was going on with her and how she affected others. She corrected herself and is still with the company.

In the end, building trust is the first and most important behavior listed because it provides the foundation for all of the others.

2. Mastering conflict. Two men who lived in a small village got into a terrible dispute that they could not resolve, so they decided to talk to the town sage. The first man went to the sage's home and told his version of what happened. When he finished, the sage said, "You're absolutely right."

The next night, the second man called on the sage and told his side of the story. The sage responded, "You're absolutely right."

Afterward, the sage's wife scolded her husband. "Those men told you two different stories, and you told them they were absolutely right. That's impossible—they can't both be absolutely right."

The sage turned to his wife and said, "You're absolutely right."[44]

No one likes taking sides in a conflict, much less being in one themselves. But conflict is not only essential to personal development and to being effective as a member of an organizational team, it is a normal part of life. That's good because, contrary to popular wisdom, conflict is *not* a bad thing for a team. In fact, when trust is present in a team, conflict becomes nothing else but the pursuit of the truth.

> When trust is present in a team, conflict becomes nothing else but the pursuit of the truth.

I remember working with leaders of an organization where one of the executives had a different idea on how maintenance should carry out its roles in the company. Most of the leaders viewed the maintenance department as being overwhelmed with open tickets to fix everyday problems and felt it needed a separate person to be in charge of long-term preventive maintenance issues. But the one executive felt strongly that the department was simply not managing its time properly and could be more aware and proactive about those long-range issues.

A detailed SWOT analysis (a study undertaken by an organization to identify its internal strengths and weaknesses, as well as its external opportunities and threats) and an on-the-ground evaluation was conducted. It was readily confirmed that the maintenance department did not have enough time to perform as required but could make improvements to better manage the time it had. The conflict resulted in the truth being exposed and the situation was rectified.

On the other hand, conflict without trust becomes politics: an attempt to manipulate others in order to win an argument regardless of the truth. One company had a supervisor who felt it was his personal duty to be in conflict with everyone. He used his position and title to manipulate people to war against one another just to get his point across. Those who worked for him only followed his direction because they were afraid of getting fired. He was eventually let go because his conflict was not healthy for the company. In the end, politicizing is almost always bad and divisive.

Naturally, disagreement during conflict brings with it a level of discomfort even among the most trusting of team members. Overcoming the tendency to run from that discomfort is one of the most important requirements for any team leader, calling to mind the familiar adage, "No pain, no gain." At one organization, there was a team member who was loyal but fed up with her supervisor's manipulative tactics. She was a stellar leader, had endured other politics in the office, and remained solid in her work performance, but she was still planning to leave the company out of frustration. Thankfully, other leadership assured her the executive's behavior would no longer be tolerated, he was removed from the company, and she chose to remain. Ultimately, she was promoted to that former executive's position, and the company is thriving under her leadership. None of it was easy or comfortable, but the result was great gain for everyone.

Avoiding discomfort in conflict only transfers greater quantities of mistrust into more groups of people throughout the organization. It is also true that different people and varying cultures participate in conflict in different ways. In many African American cultures, individuals may raise their voice levels during conversation, which may seem to some to be yelling. But it is actually a normal way they communicate during conflict. It may appear to be hostile and rude when they are in fact showing the highest level of respect for one another. The seemingly aggressive physical gesturing that may accompany such a conversation is not an indication of anger or mistrust, but of conviction of thought. Two people who are engaged in something important and who trust and care for one another should feel free to disagree, sometimes passionately.

This conflict continuum is vital, yet it necessitates the employment of two conflict tools, particularly when there is a strong cultural aversion to the discomfort conflict brings. *Mining for conflict* allows effective team leaders to establish an obligation to show dissent, knowing that if they don't, conversations that should be happening in the open will instead occur in isolated pockets and behind closed doors to the detriment of the team. While it is natural to desire consensus, the more productive approach is to get more people to speak and share their ideas so that ultimately, as Lencioni says, you "avoid the destructive hallway conversations that inevitably result when people are reluctant to engage in direct, productive debate." *Real-time permission* enables team members to coach one another instead of retreating from healthy debate. When people engaged in conflict are becoming uncomfortable with the level of discord, they should be reminded that what they are doing is necessary so they will have the confidence to continue. Once the meeting has ended, it is helpful to remind those participants that the conflict they just experienced was good for the team and not something to avoid.

Cohesive teams must take a few minutes to ensure that everyone understands each other. At the end of one executive board meeting that saw much conflict, the team decided to move forward with an updated strategic plan. Everyone around the table was asked individually if they had an issue or any questions about the new additions. Those were addressed and everyone was supportive of the plan.

3. Achieving commitment. It's been said, "You must get involved to have an impact. No one is impressed with the won-lost record of the referee."[45]

Conflict is vital—for a team cannot achieve commitment without it. Good conflict brings out what needs to be done, addresses the why, who, and what, and leads to a goal that the team can commit to and achieve. The only way to prevent bad communication is to arrive at specific agreements. The problem with communication is many times we think we have done it well when we actually did not do a good job of it at all. Neil Marten, a member of the British Parliament, was once giving a group of his constituents a guided tour of the Houses of Parliament. During the course of the visit, the group happened to meet Lord Hailsham, then lord chancellor, wearing all the regalia of his office. Hailsham recognized Marten among the group and cried, "Neil!" Not daring to question or disobey the "command," the entire band of visitors promptly fell to their knees![46] Clear communication that is both properly heard and understood is important.

At the same time, waiting for consensus in communication before taking action can lead to mediocrity and frustration. One company had a situation where they needed to change how payroll was handled and when they would pay team members. A new vendor had all the tools and support the company needed to make the changes, but not everyone was on board, and some were even fearful they might not get paid on time. So, leadership had the payroll company come in and do a demonstration of the capabilities of the new system and how it would execute and deploy the needed changes. After proper vetting, leadership decided to go forward even though one of the executives in human resources was against it. A beta test was done as a trial with a sample of team members, it worked well, and it brought consensus to the group.

It's only when people see true commitment that they will be positioned to embrace accountability.

4. Embracing accountability. To hold someone accountable is to care about them enough to risk having them blame you for pointing out their deficiencies—and on a team, peer-to-peer accountability is the primary and most effective source of being answerable and responsible to one another.

I hold myself accountable to those I lead. When there is a new project, initiative, or program that we have said we are going to do, I ask my team to hold my feet to the fire on quality, care, and delivery time of the outcomes. I developed a program of rewarding team members who did this by recognizing a winner via video each week. This was difficult to do with my very hectic schedule, but I made it happen, and the team benefited from the program.

On cohesive teams, peers confront one another without having to involve leadership. This avoids distractions and politics. Two mid-level managers of an influential organization had a disagreement concerning the process and the depth of information that should be given to those outside of their cross-function strategy group. One felt that everything discussed should be shared in its entirety. The other believed that only a summary of highlights was necessary. Without going to leadership, they came up with a solution both liked. A general summary was to be shared, with the agreement that if more info was requested, it would be given.

As part of embracing accountability, team leaders must overcome the "wuss" factor. They cannot wimp out when confronting team members on their behavior. I saw this play itself out at a large organization that had a close executive team. An executive had to confront another peer who was not taking accountability for the actions of his team. He had team members who were lagging in their duties, causing his department and others within the company to suffer. The executive told the peer about the issue and challenged him to correct things before the situation escalated and the CEO got involved.

It was hard to do. The executive and his peer had worked together for years and were friends, but in this case, the overall health of the company and its teams was more important than their personal friendship and had to be addressed. In the end, the peer could not deny the problem and truly wanted to do his best for everyone. Even though it was an uncomfortable situation, the person who was doing the offending behavior recognized it and corrected it—and no harm was done to the friendship.

It is important to distinguish between the main forms of accountability. *Measurable* accountability is easier with leaders because there are no gray areas. It is not just based on someone's judgment and theory. Measured accountability is described in specific terms (such as amount and duration) that can be easily seen. At the same time, *behavioral* accountability is more important than measurable accountability because behavioral problems almost always precede performance downturn. Most people's actions don't just show up out of thin air. The behaviors exist, but they may not have yet manifested themselves. Therefore, it is very important to address behaviors in their infancy when proper leadership can gear the individual in the right direction. It should be looked at as a strategic planning objective and addressed as soon as possible. If it isn't, the behaviors will either stay hidden or they will manifest themselves in even worse ways.

5. Focusing on results. When we work together while doing what we are supposed to do individually, then we can grow as a team and get the results we expect from our work. As each person takes responsibility for their own roles, growth and outcomes will occur. Ultimately, the whole point of building greater trust, conflict, commitment, and accountability is one thing: the achievement of results. No matter how good a team feels about itself or its outcomes, if goals are not achieved, then it is not a good team.

Cohesive teams work together to achieve a goal despite conflict and trials. They embrace the need to commit themselves to learn from one another and build the trust that will enable them to cross the finish line together. On the other hand, a non-cohesive team is only concerned with individual members looking good whether the team achieves its goal or not. Being seen as the MVP (most valuable player) of a team is great, but what really matters is winning the game. This is one reason why goals are shared across the entire team—and the only way for a team to maximize its output toward these goals is to establish the same priorities and row in the same direction.

> **Cohesive teams work together to achieve a goal despite conflict and trials.**

When consulting with a large gym company that had multiple locations, it was discovered that most of the gyms' managers were leading from their own direction and doing their own thing. If an employee went from one gym to another one in the company, they discovered that things were being done in a totally different way. My consulting team decided to visit all seven gyms, posing as customers interested in getting a membership, when we were really covertly analyzing each gym's internal processes. After a detailed study of each location, we brought all the managers together for a "best practices" seminar. The managers were not even aware that there was no continuity in processes and services between gyms. They corrected this, and it resulted in better customer experience and improved revenues.

—⊹—

An Attitude of Teamwork requires everyone to let go of ego and selfish ambition and come together with others to achieve excellence and success. When it comes to our performance, motivational speaker and self-improvement author, Brian Tracy, talks about having a positive mental attitude, and he believes that approximately 85 percent of our performance is based on our attitude. Positive mental attitude is essential to understanding ourselves in concert with understanding others to obtain maximum outcome.

DAILY DEVOTION TO ELEVATING YOUR ATTITUDE

Viktor Frankl, a survivor of Nazi concentration camps in World War II, eloquently and poignantly stated, "Everything can be taken from a man but one thing: To choose one's attitude in any given set of circumstances—to choose one's way."[47]

If you want to lead, if you want to grow, and if you want to be better, it all starts with your mindset. If you want to be rich, you can't have a poverty mentality. If you want to be the head, you can't stay the tail. Your attitude puts you in another place and carries you to an optimum state of optimism, hard work, and patience.

Therefore, you must intentionally strive each day to have an attitude that will enable you to achieve anything you want in life and to positively impact the people around you. It is not just going to happen. You must wake up every morning with a mindset that there are no bad days—only good days that will have challenges to overcome—challenges that will make you better and stronger.

Every day, I read something positive, listen to something positive, and try to find something positive in everything I see and do. You have to train your mind every single day. This is not a lifestyle that denies the realities of life or the negatives around you. Rather, it is a daily devotion in which you tool your mind so that when the challenges come (and they will), you will be able to respond in a proactive and productive manner that reflects the different attitudes I have detailed throughout this book. No matter what is going on or how things appear, when we elevate our attitude, we will not have bad days.

Join me in pursuing life—choosing *your* way—with the proper attitude to succeed.

You'll never be the same.

ENDNOTES

1 Donner Atwood. Taken from www.sermonillustrations.com
2 Today in the Word, June 11, 1992. Taken from www.sermonillustrations.com
3 Reader's Digest, January, 1992. Taken from www.sermonillustrations.com
4 Bits & Pieces, May 28, 1992, p. 15. Taken from www.sermonillustrations.com
5 Richard Conniff, "Racing with the Wind," *National Geographic*, September 1997, p. 52-67.
6 Konosuke Matsushita, founder of the PHP Institute, Inc., as quoted in Bits & Pieces, August 20, 1992, pp. 22-23. Taken from www.sermonillustrations.com
7 Bits & Pieces, May, 1991, p. 15. Taken from www.sermonillustrations.com
8 Denis Waitley. Taken from www.sermonillustrations.com
9 Max Lucado, *In the Eye of the Storm*, Word Publishing, 1991. Taken from www.sermonillustrations.com
10 Bits & Pieces, January 7, 1993, pp. 11-14. Taken from www.sermonillustrations.com
11 www.researchgate.net/publication/276002060_Rosenberg _Self-Esteem_Scale_Greek_Validation_on_Student_Sample
12 www.toppractices.com/blog/the-importance-of-self-improvement-and-personal-growth.cfm
13 Harvard Business School Online. www.online.hbs.edu/blog /post/business-skills-for-engineers
14 Adapted from www.makemeanalyst.com/ characteristics-of-scientific-method/

15 J. Stowell, Fan The Flame, Moody, 1986, p. 44. Taken from www.sermonillustrations.com

16 Jan Riggenbach, "Midwest Gardening," *Daily Herald*, May 8, 1994. Contemporary Illustrations for Preachers, Teachers, and Writers, Craig Brian Larson, p. 26.

17 Our Daily Bread. Taken from www.sermonillustrations.com

18 Bits & Pieces, August 22, 1991. Taken from www.sermonillustrations.com

19 Dr. Gary Collins, in Homemade, July, 1985. Taken from www.sermonillustrations.com

20 Bits & Pieces, March 3, 1994, p. 16. Taken from www.sermonillustrations.com

21 Christopher News Notes, August, 1993. Taken from www.sermonillustrations.com

22 "Towering Courage and Trust," p. 64. 500 Illustrations: Stories from Life for Preaching & Teaching, G. Curtis Jones and Paul H. Jones, Abingdon Press, 1998.

23 www.betterme.world/articles/examples-of-emotional-intelligence/

24 www.quora.com/What-are-some-real-life-examples-showing-emotional-intelligence

25 Ecclesiastes 5:10-12. THE HOLY BIBLE, NEW INTERNATIONAL VERSION®. Copyright© 1973, 1978, 1984, 2011 by Biblica, Inc.™. Used by permission of Zondervan.

26 George Fooshee, Homemade, Vol. 11, No. 4, (April 1987). Taken from www.sermonillustrations.com

27 Source unknown. Taken from www.sermonillustrations.com

28 Carol Jones, *The Nuts and Bolts of Investing*. Publisher, Adam Colwell's WriteWorks, March 4, 2019.

29 Angela C. Preston and Dr. Amanda H. Goodson, *Financial; Healing from the Inside Out*. Independently published, Amanda Goodson Global, February 27, 2019.

30 Bits & Pieces, May 26, 1994, pp. 18-20. Taken from www.sermonillustrations.com

31 A conversation with Jodie Foster about being a single mom in the glare of celebrity, By Tamar Laddy, Women.com, May 2000. Taken from www.sermonillustrations.com

Endnotes

32 Today In The Word, August,1989, p. 30. Taken from www.sermonillustrations.com
33 Dr. John Haggai, "Lead On!" Taken from www.sermonillustrations.com
34 Today in the Word, August, 1991, p. 13. Taken from www.sermonillustrations.com
35 Richard J. Mouw, *Uncommon Decency*, p. 117. Taken from www.sermonillustrations.com
36 George Barna, *How to Find Your Church*, pp. 104-105. Taken from www.sermonillustrations.com
37 Source unknown. Taken from www.sermonillustrations.com
38 Dwight D. Eisenhower, Bits & Pieces, September 15, 1994, p. 4. Taken from www.sermonillustrations.com
39 Bits & Pieces, September 17, 1992, p. 19-20. Taken from www.sermonillustrations.com
40 Taken from www.sermonillustrations.com
41 Charles Schultz. Taken from www.sermonillustrations.com
42 Vesta M. Kelly. Taken from www.sermonillustrations.com
43 Bill Jauss, "Catcher and Sox Both Seriously Hurt," *Chicago Tribune*, July 20, 1996, Sec. 3, p. 10; Steve Rosenbloom, "Hit and Run," *Chicago Tribune*, September 29, 1996, Sec. 3, p. 1.
44 David Moore in Vital Speeches of the Day. Taken from www.sermonillustrations.com
45 John H. Holcomb, The Militant Moderate (Rafter). Taken from www.sermonillustrations.com
46 Today in the Word, July 30, 1993. Taken from www.sermonillustrations.com
47 Taken from www.sermonillustrations.com